WILL THE REAL GOD PLEASE STAND UP

Healing Our Dysfunctional Images of God

❖   ❖   ❖

CAROLYN THOMAS, S.C.N.

PAULIST PRESS
NEW YORK ❖ MAHWAH

Library of Congress Cataloging-in-Publication Data

Thomas, Carolyn, 1936–
    Will the real God please stand up: healing our dysfunctional images of
God/by Carolyn Thomas.
        p.   cm.
    Includes bibliographical references.
    ISBN 0-8091-3208-7
    1. God—Biblical teaching.   2. God—Love.   I. Title.
BS544.T47   1990
231.7—dc20   90-48511
                                                                CIP

Published by Paulist Press
997 Macarthur Boulevard
Mahwah, New Jersey 07430

Printed and bound in the United States of America

Contents

❖   ❖   ❖

To My Mother

and

In Memory of My Father (+1974)

❖   ❖   ❖

Preface

❖ ❖ ❖

About fifteen years ago, a Chilean friend offered me a challenge that has haunted me to this day: "You are becoming a theologian. You must address the plight of the millions of people in your country who are the victims of divorce and other familial disorders that have deeply affected them and which are bound to hinder them in their relationship to God."

That observation lingered in the back of my mind, constantly churning in eager anticipation of the day when I could begin to devote some time to the project. During the interval my ministry brought me into contact with many persons of diverse ages, backgrounds and life situations. I became more and more aware of the lack of fidelity in the lives of the people with whom I worked. My experiences as a director of religious education in a parish, then as a college campus minister, and later as a seminary and university theology professor and retreat director confirmed the need for a book that deals with the authentic God whose reality Jesus came to portray for us.

My years of ministry have convinced me that the major problem is not that people do not love God; rather, the point at issue is that they have never known the real God. In not knowing this God, many persons have become bitter, while others have agonized with the mistaken idea that because of something they have done, God no longer loves them. To all the suffering people who have since confided their pain to me, as well as to those who anguished but could not verbalize their grief, I owe the courage and the desire to write this book.

First, my intention is to present an overview of the dilemma that we now face in the twentieth century and the problems it has created for many people in their relationship with God. I will show that this perplexing situation has been created by unfortunate circumstances which have given rise to an array of false images of God. Then I will use selected passages from scripture to unmask the genuine God whose love for us is never-failing regardless of our response. Subsequently, I will deal with God's boundless fidelity in forgiving us and follow with a chapter on the constant care that God lavishes upon us. Afterward I will demonstrate that God, through the writings of sacred scripture, seeks to console those who suffer from life's traumas. In conclusion I will present the call to growth that God extends to each person in order that new life may emerge from one's past, regardless of how negative it may appear.

At times I will draw on Old Testament writings as ancient witnesses to the loving, forgiving, caring and consoling God who is ours. However, since the New Testament gospels illustrate the authentic God of love who is revealed in the life and teachings of Jesus, they will be the major source for this work. The gospels are the basic foundation for our knowledge of Jesus as God-become-human who was willing to live among us and risk rejection in order that we might know the real God.

Since most of the Old Testament was originally written in Hebrew and the New Testament in Greek, I will occasionally explain the meaning of a Hebrew or Greek word which cannot be adequately expressed by an English term. Citations of scripture passages are taken from the Revised Standard Version, or from the author's own translation of the Hebrew or Greek texts with attention to use of inclusive language.

With deep gratitude I acknowledge the faithful persons who made the completion of this book possible. My nephew David Thomas, then twelve years old, was the first to give me unforgettable encouragement. He sat into the night with his dictionary reading the first pages of a scant manuscript and assured me that it would be "the best book ever written." I am also grateful to the many sisters of my congregation, the Sisters of Charity of Nazareth, especially Mary Ransom Burke, Marilyn Spink, Jean Frances Thomas and Janice Downs; to my dear friends Kathy Gaiser, Angie Laca, and Mary Anne LeSage, R.S.H.J., who all helped with proofreading and suggestions for clarifications; and last but not least, to my family and my students over the years whose questions and challenges thoroughly convinced me of the necessity of this book.

I

The Challenge

❖   ❖   ❖

I loathe my life; . . .
I will say to God, . . .
"Does it seem good to you to oppress,
to despise the work of your hands
and favor the designs of the wicked?"
(Job 10:1a, 2a, 3)

One day I shared my enthusiasm for writing this book with a friend. "Oh," inquired the woman with wide-eyed delight, "what are you writing about?" Suddenly I became hesitant, since I was aware that she had recently experienced tragic infidelity from her spouse. "Basically I am writing about God's fidelity to us." There was an instant change of expression, a blank stare into nothingness and an empty, tin-like laugh. She quipped, "The only fidelity I know anything about is Citizens Fidelity."

This pain-filled jest was an expression of deep-felt betrayal in the recesses of an anguished woman's heart. Her cynicism spoke volumes about what fidelity is not—fidelity does not lie, deceive, betray, or abandon. To the contrary, fidelity is the characteristic of a person who consistently inspires a sense of confidence and trust in another which one senses will never change. It carries with it a nuance of assurance and security which no situation will ever alter or terminate.

The experience of fidelity is foreign to the lives of many women, men and children in our society. The sources and causes are numerous and varied. The major source, yet not the only one, appears to be unhealthy family situations or a total lack of family experience. Until about thirty years ago, the stability of family life and the societal

1

norms for morality provided countless symbols of fidelity for a person. The mother and father of a family spent a lot of energy in trying to work through their problems. In many cases, in an effort to provide their children with a "normal" family life, the subsequent frustrations exploded into spouse abuse and conjugal violence. All too often, in the name of religion or purely out of good will, but to the detriment of both the couple and the children, they stayed together in spite of not being able to resolve their differences.

These efforts to be faithful have not been judged by contemporary society to be normative for today. A stable family life where a married couple remains together "until death do them part" is more the exception than the norm. Some statistics indicate that more than sixty percent of modern-day marriages end in divorce. This is not to say that the couples involved in difficult marriages should always continue together, nor that the children involved do not need a more secure and healthy environment in which to grow up. Nevertheless, the traditional symbols of fidelity provided by a stable and loving atmosphere of family life are rapidly disappearing. For many people they never did exist, or the symbols were destroyed by horrendous experiences.

In addition to unstable marriages, there is also the widespread problem of persons who have lived in families where a parent or a significant family member was alcoholic or emotionally disturbed. Many children who lived in environments with domestic violence had to develop survival techniques in order to endure psychological battering as well as physical abuse. For many of these unfortunate family victims, the traditional image of a loving mother or a loving father has been substituted by the image of a parent as tyrant or torturer and, most often, as one who acts arbitrarily instead of consistently out of love.

Numerous persons were the victims of unauthentic religious teachings. God was presented by parents or teachers, or both, as a vindictive villain who constantly spies upon us in order to catch us by surprise in whatever evil we might indulge, whether through weakness or intent. God loved only good little girls and boys, so it was advisable to keep the slate pure and untainted so as to avoid the hand of divine wrath. Such a God would be faithful only to those who merited fidelity by their good lives.

Other men and women have endured childhood sexual molestation from a parent, sibling, relative or family friend, a situation which has left these victims confused and guilt-ridden. The person who once served as role model of open, loving fidelity for a child was suddenly changed into a disgusting impostor who demanded secrecy concerning their encounters and so-called demonstrations of "grown-up" love.

How can persons whose early life experiences evolved amidst one or more of the dysfunctional family situations described above (often accompanied by distorted religious education) ever comprehend the notion of a God who is consistently faithful? How can they perceive a God whose love for us persists regardless of whether we return that love or not? The turmoil that has occurred in the minds of many of the people caught in these circumstances accounts for much of the pain that countless persons bore in their hearts as children and continue to bear silently as adults. Their experience of fidelity has been minimal, perverted, confused, and, in some cases, completely lacking.

Cognitive psychologists tell us that children are not like sponges who passively absorb whatever society pours upon them. They meet their social experiences with cognitive structures that help them interpret those experiences in a way that makes sense to them as children.[1]

How does this theory work itself out with regard to a person's concept of God? Childhood situations of instability, betrayal, abuse or distorted religious education prepare the ground for growth of false notions about God and God's relationship to us.

If life experiences have taught a person that the word "father" designates an angry, spiteful, intolerant dictator, then it is possible that when the person hears of God as "father," a negative image is evoked. A classic case is a woman who was sexually abused by her father when she was a child. For years she bore the shame and guilt in secret. As a consequence she now experiences extreme difficulty in thinking of God as a loving, caring father, one who is faithful and whose constant concern is always for her best interest and personal growth.

Many people grow up with an alcoholic parent who is gentle, loving and kind when sober, yet cruel and belligerent when intoxicated. This dysfunctional family situation often gives birth to the concept of God as one who acts according to whim instead of a God who consistently acts out of love for us.

Distorted religious education has left many people with an image of a God who is faithful only to those whose actions and attitudes merit loving fidelity. These people generally developed poor self-images as children and came to consider it unthinkable that God could love them. Any wrong-doing was viewed disproportionately; now as adults they are convinced that God has forgotten them and that the relationship, presumed to be broken, is irreparable.

The young woman Celie, in the book *The Color Purple*,[2] was only a child when she began experiencing several kinds of these personal violations. She lived through a combination of repeated rapes, alcoholic outbursts of anger, and physical abuse by her stepfather. Later she was the victim of cruel treatment by a man whom her stepfather forced her to marry. Negative experiences of males in Celie's early life were gradually transferred to her image of God, a God whom religion and society had cast into the mold of a selfish old man.

Celie began to write her feelings and the events of her miserable life in letters addressed to God. Her letters containing the horrors she had to endure vividly illustrate the barriers that an abused woman faces in perceiving God as a male who is loving and caring. One day Celie discovered beneath a floorboard a bundle of letters that her cruel and depraved husband had hidden from her. Nettie, her sister whom she loved so much and who had been separated from her during her childhood and taken to Africa, was still alive and had been writing to her faithfully over the years. Celie then began writing to Nettie instead of to a disinterested God who seemingly had never answered her anyway. In one of her letters, she told Nettie she had come to the conclusion that God was a man just like all other men she had known in her life—unfaithful, sneaky and vicious. In fact, it was God, she had decided, who had given her a degenerate stepfather after permitting her own father to go insane and be lynched. The human images Celie transferred to God had become insurmountable obstacles in a relationship that had previously meant so much to her.[3]

Many adolescents and adults, mostly victimized women but also some men, cannot relate to a male concept of God. A significant male provides a negative image that is unconsciously transferred to God who is referred to as male by a great percentage of society. Faithful love from males has not been a part of life's experiences, and neither is it a characteristic of the God they perceive.

The male image of God, however, is not the root of blockage in communication with God for all the victims of dysfunctional families. For some people, a loving and faithful mother God is equally inconceivable because of a faulty mother/child relationship.

Are persons of such unfortunate circumstances condemned to maintain forever the perverted notions or concepts of God with which their cognitive structures provided them as children? Is it possible for them to change the perceptions that were molded in the impressive years of their lives so that adulthood might become a healthy stage of growth in perceptions beyond childhood impressions?

MOVING BEYOND THE DILEMMA

Ellis and Harper[4] have identified ten irrational beliefs that severely hinder our effectiveness as human beings. One of those beliefs is that a person's past remains all-important. Because something once strongly influenced one's life, it remains forever the determining factor in feelings and behavior.[5] We cannot "uncondition" ourselves and change even if we want to.

A rational alternative to such thinking is the conviction that we are also creatures of habit and relearning regardless of how difficult that process may be. A reevaluation of past negative influences and a reinterpretation of adverse circumstances in order to adjust both conscious and unconscious perceptions is not only possible but necessary if one is to become genuinely free in one's relationships to both God and other human beings.

Celie's friend Shug had previously perceived God as an old white man, tall and gray-bearded with blue eyes and white eyelashes. That is why she had lost interest. Shug assured Celie that if she waited to find God in church, he'd be bound to show up just as she imagined—a stout white man similar to the one who worked at the bank. Words of wisdom flowed from Shug's mouth as she sought to convince Celie that God is inside everyone. Only an inward search would discover the real God.[6]

God was neither a she nor a he for Shug. She shared with Celie her own journey of moving from negative images of God. God was no longer a powerful white man but had gradually and consciously come to take on a positive image, an image which now made her happy. Nature, she told her friend, was the first channel that led to her new perception of God. Trees, birds and the air seemed to transmit a loving and caring presence of a God who was neither white nor male. Eventually, persons who were accepting, loving and kind began to convey an image of a God to whom Shug could relate. Her moment of this great discovery had been one of exuberant elation.[7]

Her friend Celie, however, was still "adrift" as she put it—still trying to chase out of her head the stubborn notion of an old white man who couldn't care less for the plight of a poor black woman. Not anything in nature—not the mystery of an unfolding blade of corn, not the beauty of wildflowers, not even the color purple which warmed her heart—absolutely nothing could distract her from the ruthless "him" that had come to represent God to her.[8]

Because Shug had also had bad experiences with men who simply used her, she told Celie that a man corrupts everything. Her own battle to replace a degenerate notion of God had been a long one. At times, she still had to struggle to adjust or rid herself of long ingrained perceptions of a false image of God in order to become free in her relationship with the authentic God. Shug warned Celie that the false god would pop up when she least expected it. He would appear on her cereal box, shout out at her from the radio, and even try to live in her mind. He would frighten her with punishment, but Shug's advice was that he should be ignored. If the image persisted, Celie should treat him as she would like to treat the evil men who had violated her. Throwing rocks had helped Shug fight off the persistent image. False images are not formed instantly, she warned, and neither would they disappear over night. The battle would require a long entrenchment.[9]

If a person's experiences have been psychologically crippling, professional counseling is most likely needed to heal the wounds that have been inflicted and lie deep within the unconscious. Today the divine healer most often uses human resources to accomplish loving, therapeutic activity. Trust in another person is frequently the first step in the process of coming to believe that there really and truly exists a God who cares and wishes to heal those who suffer from life's unfortunate circumstances. This book is not meant in any way to substitute for that need. Its purpose is to unveil the face of the authentic God who has been maligned by false images. Unauthentic masks which have been imposed upon God are repulsive and living lies about the real God shown us by Jesus.

Because we are creatures of habit and capable of relearning, I suggest two possible means of self-help: (1) prayerful imaging of a loving and faithful God such as is portrayed in the following chapters; (2) searching for symbols of faithfulness to replace the ones that do not serve to convey God's fidelity.

PRAYERFUL IMAGING OF A FAITHFUL GOD

The medical profession has discovered the value of imaging in the process of physical healing, especially in the healing of cancer. They have been most successful with children as they are uninhibited, able to let go and let another lead them. But the process is also possible for determined adults. In imaging, one is taught to imagine what the sickness looks like. Once the concrete image is formed in the mind's eye, then one imagines the white cells attacking the sickness and gradually destroying it until it is replaced by healthy cells.

A similar technique can be used as a means of self-help in efforts to change false concepts one has acquired of God. The Bible abounds with various images of God that communicate fidelity to us. To savor the deep meaning of those images, it is necessary to become like a little child, that is, to allow oneself to be led by the Spirit of God. Begin by asking God to help you to be as open as the blind beggar Bartimaeus in Mark 10:46–52. Cry out to Jesus in your heart and hear Jesus ask you as he asked Bartimaeus, "What do you want me to do for you?" Beg God to let you receive your sight, a sight that sees the true and authentic God that Jesus imaged for us when he was here among us.

With eyes closed and sitting or lying in a comfortable position, breathe slowly and deeply. Concentrate on one part of the body at a time and let each part become heavy and relaxed. Once relaxed, breathing becomes more shallow and hardly noticeable. Let some

disagreeable image of God come upon the screen of the mind—a
vicious God, a revengeful God, a God who is selective in love, or
whatever distorted image happens to clash with those that Jesus portrays in the gospels. Think of the image as modeling clay, and allow the
divine potter (Jer 18:6) to take the unauthentic clay image, transform it
and mold it into a true image of God, the image of God that we see in
Jesus, the image that Jesus came to show us.

Just as God assured the unfaithful Israelites of the Old Testament
that they could be a faithful and whole people, so is that guarantee
also our hope today. God instructed the prophet Jeremiah to go to the
potter's house and see a misshapen piece of earthenware which the
potter was refashioning into an artistic and beautiful pot (Jer 18:1-4).
Then God made a consoling promise to the sinful people:

> *O house of Israel, can I not do with you as this potter has
> done? . . . Behold, like the clay in the potter's hand, so are
> you in my hand.*
>
> (Jer 18:6)

ALTERING SYMBOLS OF FIDELITY

Another step in changing one's mistaken view of God is the alter-
ation of past symbols acquired through life's circumstances. We have
seen that for many persons, today's environment is distinctly different
from the past out of which these symbols emerged and with which
they were closely associated.[10] The transformation of a perception
that conjures up negative experiences, whether conscious or unconscious, necessitates finding alternative symbols for the concept. Certainly, as Maslow pointed out, until one's basic human needs (be they
physical or psychological) are met, it is impossible to move on to a
higher order of needs such as love and belonging.[11] Symbols derived
from one's past experiences play a major role in such progress. In his
book *Psychology and Religion*, Spinks defines symbol as follows:

> *A symbol is the expression of some theme that cannot be
> expressed in any other or better way. But if the theme should
> "evaporate" then a symbol becomes "dead," and as such can
> be said to retain only a historical significance.*[12]

The fidelity of God is not dead. The dilemma is that the symbols which in the past mediated God's fidelity to a majority of the population have never had a place in the lives of a great number of persons today. For others the symbols have died because of tragic experiences of human infidelity. In such cases new symbols are needed to perceive God as faithful, because symbols are "vitally effective means of spiritual communication and experience."[13] Distorted symbols have to be relegated to history in order to free a person to break out of the prison of the past.

What role do symbols play in the process of changing a person's perceptions? A favorable symbol tends to evoke a positive response in a person, while a negative one calls forth an unfavorable symbol as did a male figure for Celie and Shug. Words are meaningless until associated with some experience.[14] For example, to speak of a pomegranate to a child who has never seen a picture of one is like speaking to a child in a foreign language. The child has no experience upon which to form a mental image. On the other hand, if a child has previously eaten the fruit and become seriously ill shortly thereafter, it may take years to realize that in itself a pomegranate is good but not good, however, for him or for her.

Symbols play a similar role in our concept of God. Old negative symbols, which one's cognitive structures have created in the past, need not necessarily continue as symbols of God for a person if they create obstacles to the relationship. The story is told of the conversion to Christianity of a former member of the communist party. In the early days of his inquiry into Christian beliefs, the man found himself perplexed when his instructor spoke of God as "father." His own father had been anything but kind, loving, forgiving and benevolent. Therefore, the symbol "father" evoked a negative response in him. To conquer the obstacle of this inappropriate symbol, he searched his personal experience for someone who exemplified the virtues that were attributed to God by his instructor. A loving and faithful friend whom he had always addressed as "comrade" was the best human example of a person who provided him with a symbol of a faithful and loving God. Hence in his communication with God, God became "Comrade." At that particular stage of his journey, he simply had to alter the symbol for God's fidelity in order that another positive one might convey an authentic and meaningful concept to him.

As human beings with only human images as models or symbols of God, no image can possibly convey God's complete and true reality. Every symbol limps in that it limits God who is limitless love. Jesus sometimes referred to God as "Father." Since St. Paul tells us that Jesus, being God, took on our humanity through self-emptying in order to become like us (Phil 2:7), it is only natural that Jesus used symbols that were limited by his humanity to address God.

In the Jewish culture of the first century, education of the children belonged to the father,[15] so the image of "Father" for Jesus was quite appropriate to express his relationship and trust in God. However, this does not mean that "Father" must be the symbol of God for a person today if it fails to communicate an authentic, trusting relationship. Jesus himself used other symbols as well to speak of God (i.e. "shepherd," "woman," "sower of seed," "friend," etc.). The Old Testament also abounds in varied images that communicate who God is to us. They are all symbols taken from the writers' milieu which were personally meaningful in thinking of or praying to God as one faithful and trustworthy. The psalms especially provide good examples:

> *Blessed be the Lord, . . .*
> *my rock . . . my fortress,*
> *my stronghold, my deliverer,*
> *my shield, my place of refuge.*
> (Ps 144:1–2)

> *I was pushed hard, so that I was falling,*
> *but Yahweh helped me.*
> *Yahweh is my strength, my song,*
> *my salvation.*
> (Ps 118:13–14)

Today, in circumstances very different from those of the first century, each person needs to look for the symbols that evoke positive images of the authentic biblical God, a God who is faithful in love, forgiveness, care and concern for us. A universal and uniform image of God is not necessary. Of much greater importance is each individual's discovery of images that enhance one's relationship to God. That symbol will vary, depending on the positive associations of each person's background and experience (i.e. mother, father, friend, lover, etc.). Whatever the figure be, it is essential that it be one with which the individual person is comfortable, and one which acts as a bridge or a viable medium for communication with God.

In the chapter that follows, I will present biblical passages that convey the depths of God's faithful love for us. God dramatically demonstrated the depths of that love by coming to live among us as a human person. The loving, compassionate Jesus showed us the true, authentic God—faithful in loving us no matter what we do, a God whom we can love in return.

II

God Is Faithful in Loving Us

❖   ❖   ❖

Because you are precious in my eyes
and honored, and because I love you . . .
(Is 43:4)

God's faithfulness in loving us cannot be measured by standards
of human fidelity in love. If a person, for example, finds loving another
very difficult because of an experience of betrayal or lack of faithful
love, especially if it be a spouse or a good friend, it is irrational to
conclude that God reacts to one's own personal failures of love in the
same way. To do so is to reject the reality of the self-communication
of God who declares:

My thoughts are not your thoughts;
neither are my ways, your ways.
(Is 55:8)

JESUS CHALLENGES THE NOTION OF LOVE

Jesus shows us in the gospels that God does not follow the reac-
tive patterns of our selfish or psychologically conditioned human actions. In fact, frequently we find clear examples to the contrary. Jesus,
who was the human presence of God's love among us, acted counter
to the expectations of Jews who followed the norm of first century
Pharisaic thinking. For example, Jesus went far out on a limb when he
told a loyal Jewish scribe, a person learned in the Mosaic law of Israel,

12

that a Samaritan, a half-breed Jew, was to be his model for neighborliness (Lk 10:29–36). In Jesus' day, telling a Jew to imitate a Samaritan was comparable to telling an ultra-conservative modern-day Jew to imitate a member of the PLO or vice versa. Jesus saw no reason to continue the line of bitter antagonism just because his ancestors had hated Samaritans.

On another occasion, a scribe who was hostile in his attitude toward Jesus asked what he should do to inherit eternal life. Jesus responded with a counter-question: "What is written in the law? How do you read it?" (Lk 10:26). The scribe measured up to the expectations of his profession. First, he quoted a passage from Deuteronomy 6:49 which was included in the Shema, a prayer recited twice a day by every faithful Jew: "You must love the Lord your God with all your heart, with all your soul, with all your strength, and with all your mind." Then he concluded his answer with a quotation from Leviticus 19:18: "And you must love your neighbor as yourself."

Jesus accepted his answer, and we might think the incident would have closed with that, but the scribe pushed Jesus further. The scribes were always debating the question of who was an authentic member of God's covenant people, Israel. The prevailing scribal opinion was that only the pure-blooded, circumcised Jew who observed the demands of Jewish law could expect God's loving faithfulness and salvation. Jesus, however, had already disregarded the limits of their religious boundaries. To their dismay he had chosen a tax collector as a disciple and socialized with his kind (Lk 5:25–31). The scribe posed a question to Jesus that would perhaps trap him into clearly disagreeing with Israel's respected teachers of the law: "And who is my neighbor?" (Lk 10:29).

Jesus' answer came in the form of a parable (Lk 10:30–37). A man traveling from Jerusalem to Jericho was attacked by robbers. They left him stripped of his clothes, beaten and half-dead. A Jewish priest, a person of privileged status in Palestinian society, happened to pass by that way. He was probably on his way home after finishing his temple service of offering sacrifices for the people. Concerned as the priests were for their own ritual purity, he was most likely fearful of being defiled should he come in contact with blood or a corpse. Therefore, when he saw the man lying by the roadside, he did not dare go near but passed by on the other side of the road. This servant of the temple of

God let the law take preference over compassion for another person in need.

Then a Levite, another temple official and thus a person of privilege and respect in the time of Jesus, came along the same route. He was responsible for the temple's liturgy and order, so he likewise passed by on the other side of the road in order to avoid ritual defilement. Both of these pious officials, faithful in carrying out their religious practices and the observance of ritual purity, failed to respond with compassion and love to the person in need of care.

Later, a Samaritan, a member of the despised half-breed Jews living north of Jerusalem, came by the same road. This man was so moved with compassion for the badly battered person that he set about giving him first aid. He poured olive oil into his wounds to soften them and wine to sterilize them. The oils and wine were probably food staples that the Samaritan was taking home. He mounted the half-dead man upon his pack animal and took him to a public inn and put him up there. The Samaritan, one from whom no Jew would expect anything decent, went far beyond what ordinary decency would have required. He gave the innkeeper two silver pieces and instructed him: "Provide for him, and on my way back I shall reimburse you for whatever you spend over and above this" (Lk 10:35). This Samaritan man, a member of a people scorned by Jews of Jesus' day, had put at the disposal of an unfortunate Jewish victim all his material possessions—his food, his transportation, his money. Though he did not belong to God's people by birth, he had truly acted as a member of the chosen people should act. This social outcast was set forth by Jesus as a model for the Jewish scribe who was an authority on the law.

Jesus obviously did not conform to the biases of his own time. Why, then, should we force him into the mold of so-called religious experts today who deny love and compassion to others? Jesus did not hesitate to surprise and disturb the law-oriented authorities of Judaism by making persons whom they had designated as sinners or outcasts the heroes and heroines of his parables. Would he not do likewise today on behalf of those who metaphorically lie on the fringes of the institutional church all bleeding and psychologically half-dead?

CONFIRMED IN INNOCENCE

The story of Zacchaeus (Lk 19:1–10) provides a source of consolation for our own contemporary religious and social outcasts. Even the name "Zacchaeus" gives us an insight into the character of this unique little man. *Zacchaios,* the Greek form of the name, is derived from the Hebrew, *zakkai,* which means "innocent." Most often the story of Zacchaeus is interpreted as a tale of the transformation of a man's life, that is, the conversion of a sinner. Upon close examination of the story, however, we discover that Zacchaeus is the story of a good man who is only deemed to be evil by his co-religionists because he is a tax collector. His goodness as a person is affirmed by Jesus to the dismay of Israel's religious elite.

Tax collectors were the most despised of all people in the land where Jesus was born and grew to adulthood. A Jew who debased himself to collect taxes from his fellow Jews on behalf of the Roman empire was considered nothing less than the scum of society. Rome was a foreign power who took their land in 63 B.C.E., and the Romans were therefore looked upon as illegal occupants whom someday the Jews hoped to overthrow.

Zacchaeus had another strike against him. Not only was his profession despised by others—he was the *chief* tax collector in Jericho. His job consisted of farming out tax collecting rights to other men. These tax collectors in turn collected taxes on all goods passing through Jericho from lands east of the Jordan into Judea. They then turned the taxes over to their employer Zacchaeus. Consequently, his profession was extremely disgusting to the pious Jew from the point of view of his lack of loyalty to his own Jewish nation and from the economic viewpoint as well. Collecting taxes for Rome enriched and entrenched even deeper the power of the despotic Roman empire which dominated Palestine at that time, and it also increased the price of goods that the people purchased.

Tax collectors also had a reputation of being extortioners. They sometimes collected far more taxes than was necessary. This practice, in addition to their cooperation with the Romans, automatically classified them as public sinners similar to prostitutes and Gentiles. Salvation, it was thought by the "pious" Jew, could never include this debased stratum of society.

Luke tells us that Zacchaeus was rich, and that he was a short little man who could not see Jesus through the crowd. This obstacle, however, did not deter a man bold enough to accept a position such as his and dauntless enough to ignore the hostility of his Jewish compatriots. Ridiculous as it might have looked, Zacchaeus ran ahead and climbed a tree so he could have a good look at this Jesus who had a reputation for socializing with Jewish riffraff (Lk 19:3–4).

As is often the case in risk-taking, Zacchaeus' audacity paid off. When Jesus reached the place where Zacchaeus was perched up in the tree, Jesus called him by name, a practice rarely found in the gospels except in the case of close friends and associates of Jesus. "Zacchaeus" (the name meaning "innocent" or "righteous"), "make haste and come down, for I must stay at your house today" (Lk 19:5).

Luke recounts how Zacchaeus hurried down from the tree and received Jesus with great joy. The consternation and scandal of the crowds were inevitable: "He has gone to be the guest of a man who is a sinner" (Lk 19:8). Entering the house of a tax collector made one ritually unclean; the defiled person could not participate in worship without first going through ablutions and ritual cleansings with water. Ordinarily a good Jew would incur such a state of uncleanness only when it was absolutely unavoidable. Moreover, to sit at table and eat with another in first century Jewish society was a sign of one's acceptance of that person. Jesus, who had no tolerance for discrimination of any kind, took the initiative and invited himself to the home of the little man whom society had consciously ostracized. He went out of his way to publicly seek out and befriend Zacchaeus who had been excluded from the Jewish notion of religious respectability and from the elect fold of God's people.

Zacchaeus stood before Jesus and assured him that he understood his message and his concern for the poor: "Behold, Lord, the half of my goods I give to the poor; and if I have defrauded anyone of anything, I restore it fourfold" (Lk 19:8). English translations often distort the Greek from which they are translated and have Zacchaeus promising, "I will restore . . ." instead of "I restore." The future tense of the verb is a mistranslation. Zacchaeus is not simply presenting something that he intends to do in the future, but he is stating his present way of acting.[1] From this statement we may conclude that he was indeed generous with his wealth. Sharing half his goods with the poor was well beyond the twenty percent that was recognized by the rabbis as the normal amount for charity.[2]

Zacchaeus goes on to say that if he has "extorted anything from anyone," literally, "shaken anything down from anyone" (probably referring to kickbacks or intimidations by those under his supervision), "I restore it fourfold" (Lk 19:9). Zacchaeus implies that he observes the regulation of the Old Testament which required "four sheep for a [stolen] sheep" (Ex 21:37). His claim is that he has carefully observed the ethical exhortations that John the Baptist had made to tax collectors near the beginning of Luke's gospel: "Do not collect more than is legal" (Lk 3:14).

John the Baptist had not demanded withdrawal from the tax collector's profession; he had only required honesty of those who chose to practice it. Now Jesus also refuses to be swept along with the crowd and its disparaging treatment of this despised sector of society. He demonstrates the reality of a loving and accepting God who came to earth to bring good news to those who least expected it.

When Jesus calls Zacchaeus by name in Luke 19:5, he implies that Zacchaeus is indeed a just man who lives up to the meaning of his name despite the fact that his profession is disreputable in the eyes of his self-appointed judges. In spite of Jewish stereotyping, the judge who sees beyond religiosity to the depths of the human heart confirms Zacchaeus as a son of Abraham, a member of the chosen people.

Contrary to the expectations of his critics, Jesus proclaims that Zacchaeus also participates in the salvation that God had promised Israel. Men of Zacchaeus' profession were not allowed in the temple and could not participate in sacrificial ceremonies because they were considered unclean. But Jesus recognizes a goodness far more profound in this religious reject than in his self-righteous religious judges. To publicly demonstrate this reality, Jesus went to eat with the infamous tax collector. Jesus thereby made it clear that God does not allow the standards of either institutional religion or society to limit or determine the boundaries of a never failing and generous love for each individual person.

A WOMAN WHO WOULDN'T GIVE UP

Adults who suffered sexual abuse as children generally grow up as an anonymous group of society's oppressed. This is especially true if the offenders were parents or family members. In public they were treated as children, in private as lovers, a situation these children had neither the vocabulary nor the courage to reveal. In most cases the adults involved were trusted and loved before the secret encounters began. An affectionate father may have been the offspring's symbol of a loving and faithful God, or a brother may have made the biblical symbol of Jesus as brother meaningful to the child. Later the abused children involved began to feel deceived, dirty and bad. Perhaps unconsciously, but in some cases consciously, God could no longer be trusted either. This sector of society, oppressed and unknown, suffered silently in shame and disgrace as children; as adults, many of them still lack support and consolation.

Some persons, however, have been fortunate enough to get psychological counseling and have found gratifying healing. On the other hand, there are others who cannot bear to face the pain and remain permanently damaged emotionally. The devastation often spreads to the physical realm. They go from doctor to doctor, and none is able to discover the inner wound which eventually affects the whole body.

Misfortune followed by misfortune visited upon a person often leaves one feeling alone and abandoned by God as well as by people he or she loves. "How much more can I take?" is most likely a rhetorical question. The answer is clear—"No more; I have reached the end of my rope."

One of the women in the gospel, the woman with the continuous menstruation in Mark 5:25–34, experienced similar adversity. Her affliction must have remained anonymous except to those who knew her personally. Mark tells us that for twelve long years the unfortunate woman had a flow of blood. According to Leviticus 15:19–31, such a condition not only made her unclean, but it also polluted everyone and everything with which she came into contact. For twelve years anything she lay upon or sat upon was unclean. Those who touched her, her bed or where she sat had to wash their bodies as well as their clothes, and they were considered unclean until evening. What a lonely twelve years she must have endured! The gospel does not tell us whether she was married. If such was the case, she would have been deprived by law of expressing her marital love through sexual intercourse. On the other hand, if she was single, there would have been no hope for marriage which was generally expected of and by all Jewish women.

This distraught woman, moreover, was now destitute. In her desperation she had spent everything she could save going from doctor to doctor looking for a cure. Mark adds that she "had suffered much" under their treatment. The Jewish Talmud tells of remedies for such an illness that ranged from drinking wine mixed with a powder made from rubber, alum and garden crocuses to sudden shock. Regardless of the physicians' treatments, the woman only grew worse.

Despite her endless flow of blood, Jesus' reputation as a compassionate and fearless healer led the woman to venture into the crowd gathered around Jesus. Without doubt she must have feared that her uncleanness would become obvious before she could reach Jesus, and she would be shamed and disgraced before the crowd. But in her heart, the faith-filled woman was certain that she would be well again if she could but touch his garments. Why his "garments" only? The gospel does not tell us, but perhaps it was her concern for him that she might make him unclean if she touched his body. What trust she displayed in approaching Jesus in this manner, for the medical expertise of many physicians had only left her worse!

The woman's faith was indeed rewarded. The power of God active in Jesus went forth and cured her instantly. No longer would she have to hide her terrible affliction. The God whose faithfulness had led oppressed people from the scourge of pharaoh in Egypt centuries earlier was no less faithful to this daughter of Israel who had suffered enslavement from an endless twelve-year flow of blood. The woman may have intended to disappear unnoticed into the crowd, but Jesus drew attention to her. He publicly reinstated her to her rightful place within the community and society. This unfortunate woman who had endured the status of an outcast was now restored to full membership in her community. People would no longer ostracize her, and once again she could have friends.

Women and men of contemporary society who experience isolation because of secret shame can take courage from this distraught woman. There is one who can heal even the most complex cases. Most often this divine healer uses the competency of a skilled counselor so that when the hidden shame surfaces, there will be another individual to help bear the secret burden and be to the suffering person Jesus' presence as a faithful friend during the healing process.

LOVE WITHOUT RESTRICTIONS

Too often we encounter a person who feels tremendous remorse and guilt for some past sin. A woman who has an abortion, for example, may later experience such remorse and guilt that she is totally convinced that God has "marked her off his list," that God will never again love her. Many times a friend, the church, or ministers add to these persons' feelings of despair.

We know from the gospels, however, that the God whom Jesus came to show us is not selective in love. Sinner or saint, God's love does not make distinctions. Jesus lived and illustrated that non-discriminatory love by his every action. Later, in the first letter of John, the author expressed it well by his insistence that God first loved us, not because we were good or deserved it, but in spite of our sinfulness (1 Jn 4:9-12). For that reason alone, love has a chance to endure in our world.

Peter exemplifies our difficulty in understanding a God whose love embraces sinners. Luke tells us the story of Peter's all-night, bombed-out fishing expedition. Jesus came along, got into the empty boat with Peter, and told him to go out to the deep waters and lower the nets for a catch. Jesus was not what you would call an old pro at fishing; he was a teacher, so what did he know of the practical side of life? Nevertheless, tired old Peter, grumbling all the while about his long night's fruitless labors, did as Jesus suggested: ". . . but if you say so, I will lower the nets" (Lk 5:5). The results were astounding— Peter's nets started giving way and breaking so that he had to signal his fishing cronies in the other boat to come and help. They filled two boats with fish, almost to the point of sinking.

What was Peter's reaction? One would expect that he would ask Jesus to join his fishing crew. With a few catches like that, he could retire for life. But no; Peter just falls at Jesus' feet and grovels in the dirt at the thought of his many sins: "Leave me," he pleads, "for I am a sinful man" (Lk 5:8). Peter thought that because Jesus was so good, he would not want to associate with a person like him.

Jesus simply ignored Peter's protests. He was not interested in the past, and he refused to focus on Peter's sinfulness. After all, was there anyone truly without sin? Moreover, Peter had been open to the suggestion that Jesus made which brought the great catch. Despite the improbability of success after an all-night failure, Peter had rowed out into the deep waters again and made another try.

Jesus was interested in focusing on possibilities rather than on what was or what had been. He wanted to look to the future and a mutual relationship with Peter. Consequently, while Peter was down there on the ground dwelling on his sinfulness, Jesus was thinking about how they would become friends and how he really needed a person like Peter. One who recognized his or her own sinfulness was not going to be pointing a finger at the faults and failures of other people. Such a person would be able to understand the real God that Jesus taught about and could in turn take the good news of God's loving forgiveness to others.

Most people would expect Jesus to begin by reminding Peter that he would have to change if he was going to be one of his followers. But there was no scolding or chiding about his past life. Jesus simply told Peter not to be afraid and gave him a clue about his future: "From now on you will be catching people" (Lk 5:10). The beauty of it all was that Peter just took Jesus at his word. He forgot all about his sinfulness and started his internship with Jesus so he could learn about the God of whom Jesus spoke. Eventually he could begin his role of "catching people" for the kingdom of God that Jesus was beginning.

The highlight of this story is that Peter, who recognizes and acknowledges his own sinfulness, is chosen to help do the same work as Jesus. It is easy to see the reasoning behind Jesus' choice of Peter—a self-righteous person could never convince others that God is a God who takes the side of sinners. Who else but one who has experienced loving acceptance in spite of sinfulness could persuade other sinners that they too could be part of Jesus' "catching crew"?

People who experience the depths of their own sinfulness can find a rich source of encouragement in this story about Jesus and his attitude toward sinners. The fact that we have sinned, as Jesus has shown us, need not discourage us from turning to him. To the contrary, the acknowledgement of our sinfulness can open us to the invitation of Jesus who loves us and who can turn our failures into occasions of bringing others to him. The further down we have fallen, the greater the void we have to be filled with God's love and greater the chance we have of unmasking the real God for other people.

Is God Fair?

"If you do your part, you can be sure that God will come through with a fair deal." People who think like this would argue that God is a fair God. According to this way of reasoning, God is one who plays the game according to the same rules by which human beings play, that is, a God who gives us what we deserve. But that is certainly not the God about whom Jesus taught. In light of Jesus' teachings, the authentic God is not a fair God at all judging by human standards of fairness.

Jesus gave us a good insight into the "fairness" of God in the parable he told about a vineyard owner hiring workers (Mt 20:1–16). In the early morning hours he went out and found some people who agreed to work for him all day for a denarius (the general day's wages in Jesus' time). About nine o'clock the vineyard owner went out to the marketplace a second time and found more idlers who agreed to work for the same wages given the first group. Again he went out at noon, at three o'clock and once more at five o'clock. Each time he took others in to work because no one else had hired them.

When the workday ended, the vineyard owner had his cashier call in the workers, and pay each one a denarius, beginning with those who started work at 5:00 P.M. on to those who began early in the morning. When the early workers walked up for their pay, they were disappointed and shocked that they did not receive any more than those who worked only one hour. They had worked through the heat of the day which was no small feat in the scorching mid-day temperatures of Palestine. These others had done only an hour's work in the cool of the day, yet they received exactly the same pay. Complaints began to bombard the owner. Hadn't they worked harder? In all fairness, they thought that they deserved much more than the late-comers. Their assessment of the situation was that their employer was unfair.

The vineyard owner, however, had a different way of looking at things. The early workers had agreed on a denarius. Why should they begrudge those who had received the same payment for less work? He had surely not been unjust to those who worked all day. He paid them exactly what they agreed upon in the morning, and it was a fair day's wages.

Jesus maintains that God deals with us as the vineyard owner dealt with his hired hands. Ours is a loving God who does not keep count according to human rules of fairness but goes far beyond. God's generosity to us is boundless and not limited by our late repentance. Like the vineyard owner, God seeks us out even to the last hour so as to share eternal life with us. Those who come last are loved as dearly as those who were always faithful.

III

God Is Faithful in Forgiving Us

❖   ❖   ❖

God does not deal with us according to our sins.
(Ps 103:10)

Forgiveness is often a vague and unfamiliar concept in the summation of childhood and adult experiences of many people. How can a person think of God as one who forgives if forgiveness has not been among one's life experiences? Parents who convey to their children a sense of personal rejection when they displease them lay the groundwork for future transferal to God of feelings of harsh abandonment. In later years of maturity, God becomes revengeful when they sin and gets back at them through life's hardships and misfortunes.

"God is going to get you!" Words such as these smolder in the depths of many hearts. For a desperate parent they were a harmless warning that issued forth from an arsenal of self-defense and a need for a moment's peace. While the threat secured a short-lived respite from noise and mischief, there was a simultaneous, unconscious buildup of defense in an innocent mind against a vengeful, tyrannical God. There is little wonder that many adults refer to God as "the man upstairs." They feel far removed from an alien God who has little interest in their lives except to execute the role of both prosecutor and judge of their actions.

An unrelenting spouse who maintains grudges because of hurts in marriage may likewise pave the way for a partner's lack of trust in God's forgiveness. A husband or wife who refuses pardon to the other fails to image the forgiveness of the God whose love their marriage commitment is supposed to exemplify. For the rejected party, God often becomes a vicious character who waits for every opportunity to get even.

Situations in which forgiveness has not been modeled or where it has been blatantly denied frequently set the stage for a distorted view of God. Just as some significant individual failed to forgive, so also does God become the object of mistrust.

A UNILATERAL DISARMER

The concept of a God who is so generous in forgiving us is one that human beings have difficulty comprehending. Biblical writings reflect various stages of belief in God's limitless mercy. The Old Testament abounds in stories of and allusions to God's fidelity in forgiving us. One of the most well-known narratives is the story of the flood that reflects the ancient world's belief that a flood had destroyed the earth at one time. According to the story in Genesis, all human beings except Noah and his family, and all creatures except two of every kind, were wiped off the earth. Afterward God made an agreement or covenant with Noah never again to destroy the earth and living things by water:

> *This is the sign of the covenant which I make between you and me and every living creature. . . . I set my bow in the clouds over the earth and it shall be a sign of the covenant. . . . When I bring clouds over the earth and the bow is seen in the clouds, I will remember my covenant . . . and the waters shall never again become a flood to destroy all flesh.*
> (Gen 9:12–15)

In Hebrew, the original language of the book of Genesis, the word used for "bow" is *qesheth*. In other places in the Old Testament that word is translated into English as "bow of war." If the author intended to convey the notion of a weapon of war instead of the more familiar translation of "rainbow,"[1] then the bow was a sign that God wished to forgive us and to be at peace with us.

The Hebrew author may have borrowed the idea for the story from an ancient Babylonian myth of creation in which "bow" is also used in the sense of "bow of war." In the myth the god Marduck destroys Tiamat, the god of the abyss, and then hangs his bow in the heavens as a warning to all people of his terrible might and power. In the flood story in Genesis 9, the writer sets up a dramatic contrast between Yahweh, our God, and the Babylonian god Marduck. While Marduck hung his bow in the heavens to engender fear in the people, Israel's God placed a bow there as a sign of covenant or agreement with all of creation: "When I see it," God declares, "it will remind me of the everlasting covenant" (Gen 9:11). The "bow," then, is not a threat to us; it is a symbol of God's desire to always be faithful in forgiving us.

On the other hand, if the author intended to convey the notion of a rainbow[2] instead of a "bow of war," it still remains a reminder of God's fidelity. God will never again destroy the earth; that is, God will never desecrate the ground of relationship with us or let any barrier come between us. We will always be able to walk with God upon familiar terrain. The ground between us and this loving, forgiving God is safe, and we need not be afraid that God will break relationship with us because of what we have actually done or what we feel we have done. We may turn away from God, but God will never turn away from us.

The Old Testament story of the encounter of Moses with God on Mount Sinai paints an ancient portrait of God as faithful in forgiving us. Moses went up to a mountain, often a place of God's self-revelation in the Bible, and spoke confidently with God in spite of the repeated acts of infidelity on the part of the people he was leading. God had led them safely from the Egyptian pharaoh's oppressive hand. When they reached the expansive desert beyond Egypt, they became dubious and murmured against Moses and his brother Aaron. Were not the pots of meat in Egypt to be preferred to the apparent barrenness of the desert? God, in turn, patiently rained down food for them, gave them water from a rock, and delivered them from the hostile nations surrounding them (Ex 34). Yet, in spite of God's unfaltering fidelity, they doubted God's faithfulness to them and constructed a molten calf to worship as their god.

The storyteller portrays God as becoming very angry and threatening to destroy the Israelites. But Moses, in a humorous and intimate way, reasons with God. The Egyptians would surely gloat and sneer at a God who saved the people from their enemies only to destroy them in the desert. After all, hadn't God promised their ancestors that they would become a great nation? Their annihilation would put God in a bad light. The narrator states that God listened to Moses and decided not to wipe out that ungrateful people (Ex 32:9–14).

Our early religious ancestors, whose perceptions of God are reflected by a combination of ancient writings, did not think of God as a vindictive tyrant ready to strike the people to get even with them for their failures. Rather, they perceived God as a personal God, as the book of Exodus, for example, verifies: God spoke with Moses "face to face as a person speaks with a friend" (Ex 33:11); Moses asked God to accompany them on their journey, and God readily complied (Ex 33:15–17); Moses spent forty days and forty nights alone with God, conversing on a mountain (Ex 34:28–29). That is hardly a portrait of an indifferent, unforgiving, harsh God.

JESUS UNMASKS THE REAL GOD

As with many persons throughout history, the Jews of first century Palestine also had trouble comprehending the magnitude of God's forgiveness. In spite of his critics' disapproval, Jesus attests by his words and actions in all four gospels that God is a compassionate and forgiving God. That message, however, did not please those to whom observance of the law of Moses was more important than human compassion and forgiveness.

Before Jesus came, there was John the Baptist. John had lived a strict life void of comforts in the desert. He came forth preaching repentance which involved justice and a concern for the well-being of every person. Luke tells us that the tax collectors, the worst of Jewish outcasts, listened and did as John had pleaded in his admonitions. The Pharisees and scribes, on the other hand, called John a madman and rejected the prophet's message. Herod had John imprisoned to silence him (Lk 3:1–19). Mark and Matthew give us the gory account of the beheading of John by Herod with the display of his head on a platter at a banquet (Mk 6:17–29; Mt 4:3–12). It wasn't safe to speak of justice and give sinners and the unclean of Jewish society hope for salvation.

Then Jesus came among us and, in contrast to John the Baptist, lived a free and normal life. The self-righteous religious leaders likewise refused to listen to Jesus because his code of behavior and ethics did not coincide with theirs. In Jewish culture of Jesus' day, to sit at table with a person was to admit one's unconditional acceptance of the person. Jesus demonstrated that acceptance by sitting at table and sharing meals with people who were ostracized and held in contempt by society. He was criticized by his opponents and was accused of being "a glutton and a drunkard, a friend of tax collectors and sinners" (Lk 7:34). But Jesus would not compromise his message of God's love and forgiveness. He compared his critics to a group of spoiled children sitting in a marketplace, sulking because another group of playmates refused to play their games. They call out to the resistant group:

> *"We piped you a tune but you did not dance;*
> *We sang you a funeral song but you did not wail."*
> (Lk 7:32)

Such was Jesus' way of saying that John's ascetic life and message of repentance and justice accompanied by a threat of the impending wrath of God had been rejected by the self-righteous religious leaders. They had not liked John's strict way of life, but preferred that he be joyous. Then Jesus came and lived an entirely different style of life. His was a joyful manner of living accompanied by a message of repentance and justice which focused not on God's wrath but on God's love and forgiveness. But neither was Jesus and his message acceptable to those who believed that God's salvation was reserved for a ledger of law-abiders. The self-righteous critics had cast God into a mold of their own making and refused to open their minds and hearts to God's good news to us proclaimed by Jesus.

A SINFUL WOMAN TAKES A RISK

Persons burdened with a sinful past often cannot see beyond the dark, invisible curtain drawn by society or established religion to separate them from the so-called "righteous" people. These saddened individuals who have been refused forgiveness can find courage to lift their heads again if they but peer through the window of Luke's gospel and ponder the scene of the sinful woman who anoints the feet of Jesus.

Following the story of Jesus' meal with a tax collector, Luke tells us that Simon, a Pharisee, invited Jesus to eat with him (Lk 7:36–50). While Jesus was at table, a well-known sinner of the town heard that he was dining in the Pharisee's house. She entered the dining room of an all-male circle and stationed herself behind Jesus at his feet. This repentant woman cried so hard that she moistened his feet with tears and then proceeded to dry them with her hair. She kissed his feet, a reverence which was generally paid only by disciples to respected teachers, or by an accused murderer grateful to his lawyer for his acquittal. The woman then anointed the feet of Jesus with ointment.

Since we have heard the story repeatedly, we may fail to recognize the courage of this woman sinner. Recognition by Simon that she was a sinner may indicate that she was a prostitute who had been betrayed time and time again by false demonstrations of love. Perhaps that is the reason Simon thinks that if Jesus were a prophet, he would know what kind of woman was touching him.

Prostitutes were treated as outcasts by the religious establishment of Israel in the time of Jesus. What, then, was this well-known sinner doing in Simon's house in the first place? Did she enter from the street uninvited? If so, why did Simon not order her to leave? The common practice was that Pharisees did not associate with sinners. Could it be that she was a "secret visitor" of Simon's? Luke does not answer these questions in his account of the story. Nevertheless, it leaves one to ponder the issue because later in the story, Jesus compares her demonstrations of love with Simon's lack of concern for him. Entering the dining room of a Pharisee during a meal for an invited guest required courage undaunted by human respect. Yet for reasons not recounted by Luke, the woman found in Jesus a man whom at last she could trust.

The Pharisee host capitalizes on the incident to evaluate the credibility of Jesus: "If this man were a prophet, he would have known who and what sort of woman this is who is touching him, for she is a sinner" (Lk 7:39). Jesus knows Simon's thoughts and is aware that his reputation is at stake. However, Jesus will not put his own self-esteem above his concern and love for a person whom society scorns and deprives of all sense of worth.

Jesus tells Simon the Pharisee a parable of two debtors in which both are forgiven by the person who loaned them money. One of the debtors owed a great amount, the other a small one. Simon is asked to judge which man loved the money-lender more. "The one for whom he canceled the greatest debt," Simon answered (Lk 7:43). Jesus affirms his answer, but he reminds Simon that he had received no such demonstration of love from him when he entered his house as he had received from this woman:

> *Then turning toward the woman he said to Simon, "Do you*
> *see this woman? I entered your house, you gave me no water*
> *for my feet, but she has wet my feet with her tears and wiped*
> *them with her hair. You gave me no kiss, but from the time I*
> *came in she has not ceased to kiss my feet. You did not*
> *anoint my head with oil, but she has anointed my feet with*
> *ointment. Therefore I tell you, her sins, which are many, are*
> *forgiven, for she loved much; but one who is forgiven little*
> *loves little.*
>
> (Lk 7:44–47)

From Jesus' point of view, both Simon and the woman are sinners. They differ, however, as in the parable: the sinful woman has loved much and therefore is forgiven much. Simon did invite Jesus to his house, but unlike the sinful woman, he showed no indications of kindness and love. Instead of examining his own way of life, Simon takes a self-righteous stance as judge of Jesus' credibility.

Jesus assures the woman, "Your sins are forgiven. . . . Your faith has saved you; go in peace" (Lk 7:50). This woman's sinful past is not to burden her. The peace he gives her is that of the Old Testament *shalom,* meaning "to be whole" or "complete," an experience of well-being that comes only from God. That was a peace of which no one could deprive her, not even the religious leaders of her nation.

Sometimes we get the impression that modern leaders of established religion fear that the reputation of their traditions will be jeopardized if persons outside the boundaries of "acceptable" morality are received into the fold with love and compassion. If the church is truly to be the abiding presence of the Lord in history, it has to model God's faithful forgiveness as effectively today as it was exercised by Jesus in the first century. The institutional church is challenged to be as daring as the Lord of that church who never considered his own reputation to be more important than a person in need of compassion. He dared to make sinners and outcasts the heroes of his parables (i.e. Lk 10:29–36; 18:9–14), and he himself associated with the despised persons of Jewish society under the disdaining eyes of the scribes and Pharisees.

JESUS RESTORES PETER'S SELF-WORTH

Many people who have been unfaithful in their relationship with God assume that God has broken relationship with them. They perceive themselves as unworthy of forgiveness after having sinned. Moreover, they think of themselves as bad persons and believe they deserve whatever misfortunes befall them. These sincere but misinformed persons presume that their sinfulness has created an irreparable breach between them and their God.

The gospel of John gives us the touching description of Jesus' response to Peter after the disciple's denial of him. The story vividly demonstrates the faithfulness of the loving God whose reality Jesus shows us (Jn 21:1–18). To understand the seriousness of Peter's breach of friendship with Jesus, one has to remember that Peter was one of Jesus' closest friends and associates; he was one of the twelve and the spokesperson for them in the fourth gospel. Yet he was the only one of them who is said to have denied that he was a follower of Jesus.

Peter's denials in John's gospel are highlighted by an incident earlier in the narrative when Jesus said, "Where I am going, you cannot follow me now but you will follow me later" (Jn 13:36). At that point, Peter declared his radical faithfulness to his Lord: "Why can't I follow you now? I will lay down my life for you" (Jn 13:37). When the chips were down, however, and Peter feared for his own safety, he denied any acquaintance with Jesus. While Jesus was inside Caiaphas' house being interrogated by the high priest and witnessing to the truth of his real identity, Peter cowered on the outside denying that he knew the person who had claimed to be the truth. Not only once did Peter deny his association with Jesus, but three times. The intervals between these denials in John's gospel emphasize his culpability. The last two times, at least, were not spur-of-the-moment weaknesses. Peter had had time to reflect on his denials, and they clearly bore the tag of decision. When it came to standing by his friend and master in time of trouble, Peter appears to be a weak-kneed coward.

After the narrative of Jesus' death and resurrection, John's gospel follows with a story of Jesus' appearance to his disciples on the beach at the Sea of Galilee during a fishing venture (Jn 21:1–18). Peter had decided to return to his old occupation of fishing, and some of the other disciples of Jesus had joined him. They had fished all night and caught nothing. Suddenly Jesus was standing on the beach calling out for them to cast the net to the right side of the boat where they would find fish (Jn 21:6). In spite of the fact that they themselves were the expert fishermen, even if a bit out of practice, they did as Jesus suggested and made a great catch—one hundred and fifty-three fish!

Biblical scholars are uncertain whether the number one hundred and fifty-three has symbolic meaning, but in "The Testament of Zebulon" in *The Testament of the Twelve Patriarchs,*[3] an apocryphal work not contained in the Christian or Jewish scriptures, a great catch of fish was a sign of God's favor. Such may also be the case in John's story of the disciples' big haul. Despite Peter's denials and the other disciples' abandonment of him, Jesus continues to love them with gracious and bountiful generosity as demonstrated by the overflowing net of fish. His concern is not at all for their lack of fidelity in friendship to him; rather, his consideration is for the disciples themselves whom he loves in spite of their failures.

When "the disciple whom Jesus loved" announced that it was the Lord, Peter put on his clothes, "for he was stripped for work, and he sprang into the sea" (Jn 21:7). We have generally assumed that Peter jumped into the sea and swam to shore in his eagerness to be with Jesus. Since John doesn't give us a reason for Peter's action, it is impossible to know for certain its significance. It might very well be a symbolic gesture.

The symbolism of the sea may provide a key to understanding Peter's plunge into the water. In the Old Testament the sea is often viewed as a place of evil and chaos, as it was in the ancient myths. For example, in Job 38:8–11 it is a monster whom God has restrained. In the book of Revelation in the New Testament, the sea is one of the hostile elements that has no place in the new creation: "the sea was no more" (Rev 21:1). The writer is saying by means of symbol that evil will have no place in the new creation which God has prepared for us.

When Peter hears that it is the Lord, he clothes himself just as did Adam and Eve in the story in Genesis 2 when they experienced their guilt. He then jumps into the sea, a symbol of evil and chaos, where he feels at home in his guilt. Peter thus expresses his sense of guilt for having deserted his friend in Jesus' time of great need. He has lost his self-esteem and judges that Jesus feels about him the way he feels about himself.

On the beach, however, Jesus has breakfast prepared and waiting for the disciples. "None of the disciples dared ask him 'Who are you?' They knew it was the Lord" (Jn 21:12). How could they be so sure it was Jesus? Without doubt they were convinced that the disinterested love and friendship in the aftermath of denial and abandonment could only be that of Jesus whom they had followed and knew so well. Such boundless forgiveness was the compassionate and unmistakable trademark of the one with whom they had walked as intimate friends.

Peter's encounter with Jesus in this scene is similar to encounters of Jesus with other sinners to which Peter has heretofore been witness. Like the Samaritan woman (Jn 4:1–32), Peter now stands defenseless in his sinfulness. Contrary to human expectations, Peter not only experiences loving forgiveness from Jesus but also further trust.

Jesus gives over the care of his flock to this fragile and weak disciple, but not before some preliminary clarifications. Three times he asks Peter if he loves him, and three times Peter affirms his love, just as three times before he had denied that he even knew Jesus. Most likely the repeated question is meant to recognize the denials and to help Peter realize that he does indeed love his Lord in spite of his failures. Peter is to understand that love rather than guilt is the basis for discipleship, forgiveness and service to his flock. He had denied his discipleship when he was under the accusing eyes of the Jerusalem authorities in a terribly threatening situation. Painful as that reminder may be, Peter is to accept the fact that he is still considered a disciple as well as a friend, and that Jesus continues to trust him despite his lack of support and loyal friendship on the eve of his death.

Broken relationships can be healed, especially those with the risen Lord. Jesus often testified that he came to show us the face of God. The God he revealed to us is a God who is eager to heal whatever

violations of relationship we may think have created a wall of alienation between us. This authentic God waits for us as he waited for the
disciples on the beach, not to accuse and weigh us down with further
guilt, but to forgive and to reassure us of an unfailing love. If Peter
could be forgiven and reinstated to a relationship even more intimate
than before, the God whose face was shown us by Jesus will also
forgive whatever infidelity might be ours when we acknowledge our
sinfulness with sorrow.

A Forgiven and Forgotten Past

How often we tend to allow the past to intimidate us in our
relationship with God! It is as if we want to punish ourselves for
something we did, and one way to do that is to resign ourselves to an
alienated position in relation to God. This self-imposed estrangement
does not correspond with God's desire for intimacy with us. Jesus
portrayed for us a God who does not concentrate on our past. The
authentic God lives rather in the present and is one for whom the past
serves only to make forgiveness of us a shocking proof of the incredi-
ble depths of divine love for us.

In the gospel of Luke, Jesus is mocked while hanging on the
cross, not by both thieves who are crucified alongside him as in the
gospels of Mark and Matthew, but only by one of them. The other
criminal chides his fellow wrongdoer:

> *"Do you not fear God, since you are under the same sen-
> tence of condemnation? And we indeed justly; for we are
> receiving the due reward of our deeds; but this man has done
> no wrong." And he said, "Jesus, remember me when you
> come into your kingdom."*
>
> (Lk 23:40–42)

The condemned man asked for nothing specific from Jesus, nothing
that a criminal shouldn't ask of an innocent fellow sufferer; he simply
requests that he be remembered.

The past of one's life is for Jesus only a stepping stone for a
deeper loving relationship. Thus Jesus' response to the thief leaves no

room for the man to wallow in guilt over something he cannot undo. He accepts the man who has turned to him, not as a hopeless criminal, but just as he is at that moment: "Today you will be with me in Paradise" (Lk 23:43). Only the man's present was of interest to Jesus.

In Paul's letters to various Christian communities which are preserved in the New Testament, we find a good example of a person who refused to grovel in the sinfulness of his past life. Paul acknowledges in his letter to the Galatians that before his experience of the risen Lord, he persecuted "the Church of God violently and tried to destroy it" (Gal 1:13). But once Paul realized he was wrong, he repented and faced the future totally dependent upon God's mercy and grace. Instead of allowing his past to become an obstacle to his growth in relationship to Christ, Paul used it as a basis for a tireless ministry in bringing others to know the authentic God about whom he had been mistaken before his conversion.

In contrast to Paul, we sometimes try to pull God down into the mire of an entangled past with us. It may be that we create a God to our own image, or that we set ourselves up as judges of another person and seek to make the past of someone else all-important to others and to God. To any of us would-be-judges, Jesus says:

Judge not and you will not be judged; condemn not, and you will not be condemned; forgive, and you will be forgiven; give, and it will be given to you; good measure, pressed down shaken together, running over, will be put into your lap. For the measure you give will be the measure you get back.

(Lk 6:37–38)

A WOMAN CONDEMNED BY A KANGAROO COURT

The compassionate forgiveness of God is again dramatically illustrated by Jesus in the story of a woman whom the scribes and Pharisees brought to Jesus and accused of committing adultery (Jn 8:1–11). Without doubt this woman in the Jewish society of the first century had little hope of acquittal. "Master," they say, "this woman was caught in the very act of adultery, and Moses has ordered us in the law to condemn women like this to death by stoning. What have you to say?"

From what is known of the justice system of first century Palestine, we sense that something underhanded is going on here. A sentence of condemnation had to come from the Jewish Sanhedrin. However, under Roman law, not even the Sanhedrin had the right to put a person to death; that was the prerogative of the Roman official to whom the Sanhedrin was subordinate.

Why then did the scribes and Pharisees bring the sinful woman to Jesus for an opinion? As far as they were concerned, Jesus was only one of many itinerant preachers of his day who had no authority to act in the matter. Obviously they wanted to trap him. If Jesus advocated compassion for her, he would put himself in the category with sinners who have no regard for the law of Moses. In that case he could be in serious trouble with the Jewish Sanhedrin. On the other hand, if he conceded that they must stone her, he would show contempt for the law of Rome, which was an even greater perilous endeavor. What will Jesus do? He could protect his rabbinic reputation and call for stoning as the Mosaic law mandated. Jesus' reputation hangs in jeopardy.

The trapped woman stands all alone in disgrace with little to hope for from a Jewish teacher of her day. The accusers say that she was "caught in the act of adultery." Why then does this woman stand by herself in the midst of this circle of self-righteous men? Clearly a man had to be involved in the action if the woman was caught in adultery. The law of Moses prescribed death for both the man and the woman when such was the case (Lev 20:10). Nevertheless, it appears that the man involved in this instance walked away scot-free. Unlike men of that time and society, women had no legal rights. Moreover, categorized as a public sinner, she is an outcast of society and despised by the scribes and the Pharisees. Would Jesus also follow suit and save face by condemning her?

The gospel writer tells us that Jesus bent down and began to write on the ground. We do not know what he wrote; he may have been simply doodling on the ground to show his indifference to their presence. When they continue to question him, however, Jesus responds with an unexpected cleverness: "The man among you who has no sin—let him be the first to cast a stone at her" (Jn 8:7). Because of their deceitful pretension of acting out of respect for the law of Moses, they had unwittingly placed themselves together with the woman in the category of sinners.

One by one the outwitted scribes and Pharisees begin to leave until the frightened and humiliated woman stands alone face to face with Jesus. He does not deny her guilt, for he would never condone infidelity in marriage as he carefully demonstrated in his encounter with the Samaritan woman at the well (Jn 4:17–18). His compassion, however, rings true in his dialogue with her: " 'Woman, where are they? Has no one condemned you?' She said, 'No one, Lord.' And Jesus said, 'Neither do I condemn you; go and do not sin again' " (Jn 8:11).

Like the accusers in the story, there always seem to be some people who appear to survive on discerning and judging the hearts of others. Judgments by individuals both within and outside the church have left many persons lonely and heavily laden with guilt. Viewed from the perspective of Jesus' treatment of the woman caught in the act of adultery, one cannot forget that his forgiveness was extended not to the denouncers but to the one denounced. Those who stood in judgment of the woman chose to walk away from Jesus' presence once they realized that he perceived the depths of their own secret sinfulness. The woman, however, stripped of her self-respect, discredited as an unfaithful wife, and relegated by the religious elite to the level of society's scum, stands defenseless before the discerner of all truth. She does not slink away into oblivion as did her accusers, and neither does she make excuses or pretensions. She waits in naked silence and is clothed with loving forgiveness.

The gospel of Luke gives us a summary of Jesus' teachings on judging others: "Be merciful, even as your God is merciful" (Lk 6:36). Rich in meaning in its biblical origin, the word "mercy" includes nuances which the English translation fails to convey. In the Old Testament, "mercy" implies a mutual relationship between God and Israel which was initiated by God. Love, fidelity and pardon were aspects of mercy which the people could expect from God even when they were not faithful in return. Just as God, therefore, is faithful, loving and forgiving even when we do not deserve it, Jesus asks this same unconditional mercy of us in dealing with one another.

GOD IS NOT A BOOKKEEPER

Peter wanted to know to what extent we are expected to forgive others. He asked if seven times were enough. Jesus proceeded to tell a parable (Mt 18:21–35) which he concluded with a rather frightening statement about how we ourselves tailor God's forgiveness of us.

The parable concerns a king whose servants owed him money. One of them owed the king "ten thousand talents," the equivalent of about one million denarii, which in turn would amount to a man's wages for 2,777 years. Obviously, that was quite a debt, and certainly one impossible to pay. Such a huge amount suggests that the man was the king's tax collector. According to Roman law under which most of the known world of the first century lived, a person who owed a debt had a thirty-day period of grace to pay debts that were due. The king in the parable, however, disregards the law and immediately orders the servant to be sold "along with his wife and children and all that he had and payment be made" (Mt 18:25). The servant implores the king for a deferment, which was rightfully his by law, after which time he would pay the whole debt. The king feels so much compassion for the man that he releases him immediately and wipes out the entire debt. Generous pardon was the only hope for the man, for he could never have paid such an insurmountable sum of money.

One would think that a person who had experienced inconceivable mercy, compassion and generosity would in turn act accordingly to those who were indebted to him or to her. Not so with the servant in this parable! He went out and found a fellow servant who owed him only one hundred denarii, the equivalent of about one hundred days' wages, and he demanded immediate payment. That was a small sum compared with the amount that the first servant had owed the king. Nevertheless, he had the man imprisoned until he could pay the entire debt. When the king heard of the forgiven servant's lack of compassion for his fellow debtor, he called him in and revoked the pardon he had granted the wicked servant.

Our debts of infidelity to God may be compared to the unimaginable debt of the wicked servant. Yet, regardless of the length of time we allow ourselves to turn away in anger, shame or indifference, God willingly and with great compassion forgives us no matter what the sin or sins may be. Forgiveness, however, is not earned by us; it is God's gratuitous gift. As the parable illustrates, the only way we can cut ourselves off from God's forgiveness is to refuse to forgive those who offend us.

Persons who anguish from past experiences, especially victims of incest, abuse, or spousal infidelity, sometimes feel guilty and conclude that they "fall between the cracks" of God's forgiveness. The pain is too great and too deep, and they may even feel that they do not wish to forgive the offender. That is where the divine healer can enter in and cure the wounds from their very depths, a process which generally occurs gradually and with the help of a skilled counselor. Meanwhile, God knows the deep roots of the pain, the dryness of heart one feels, and understands as well the time it takes to heal. The psalmist in the Old Testament assures us of God's loving patience:

> *The Lord is gracious and merciful,*
> *slow to anger, and abounding in steadfast love.*
> (Ps 145:8)

God's promise to Israel through the prophet Ezekiel is also God's personal commitment to each of us:

> *A new heart I will give you and place a new spirit within you,*
> *taking from your bodies your stony hearts and giving you*
> *natural hearts.*
> (Ez 36:26)

The climactic moment occurs when the wounded and scarred person can begin to pray as Jesus did for those who were responsible for his death on the cross: "Forgive them, for they know not what they do" (Lk 23:34).

IV

God Is Faithful in Caring for Us

❖   ❖   ❖

God is merciful and gracious,
  slow to anger and abounding in steadfast love.
                            (Ps 103:8)

A devastating experience such as divorce or infidelity on the part of a loved one often leaves a person so shattered that one's needs are numerous and even unclear. At the same time, God appears to be non-existent or far away and unaware of what is happening. Prayer becomes seemingly useless, impossible, or extremely difficult.

The sense of being alone and abandoned by God especially when things are rough is reflected by a person's prayer of desperation in an Old Testament psalm, a prayer of one drained of all self-defenses. The prayer that came forth from Jesus' lips in his cry of agony on the cross in Mark's gospel is from that psalm:

My God, my God, why have you forsaken me?
Why are you so far from helping me, from the words
  of my groaning?
O my God, I cry by day, but you do not answer;
  and by night, and I find no rest.
                            (Ps 22:1–2)

Frequently after one has come to the end of the tunnel of intense suffering, reflection on the past affords one the opportunity to look back and realize how so many of our unconscious needs were taken care of—a friend came into our lives at just the right moment, or something unexpected occurred that suddenly made the pain bearable. Only then can we utter the rhetorical question, "Was God really so absent after all?" In another of the Old Testament psalms, we sense the relief of a person who had a similar experience and at long last found an oasis in the midst of trials:

> *I waited patiently for God;*
> > *God inclined to me and heard my cry.*
> *. . . drew me up from the desolate pit,*
> > *out of a miry bog,*
> *and set my feet upon a rock,*
> > *making my steps secure.*
>
> (Ps 40:1–2)

When the ancient Israelites felt abandoned and forsaken by God, they did not hesitate to express it. Likewise when things began to go well, they often cried out their feelings of relief with similar deep passion of gratitude.

LIKE A TENDER PARENT

To understand the real God whom Jesus came to show us, it is helpful to consider some of the images of God in the Old Testament. The people of ancient Israel felt as we do occasionally—deserted or abandoned by God in their trials and tribulations. The prophets, however, who spoke God's word to the people assured them that they were never forsaken. To the contrary, they were constantly accompanied and pursued during both good and bad times by an anxious, loving and caring God. Just as God spoke to the people through the prophets, so too does that same God speak to us, anguish with us and for us as we struggle, and sometimes muddle, through pain-filled days, months, and often years:

> *I have called you by name, you are mine.*
> *When you pass through the waters, I will be with you;*
> > *and the rivers shall not overwhelm you;*
> *When you walk through fire you shall not be burned,*
> > *and the flames shall not consume you.*
>
> (Is 43:1b–2)

Psalm 139 is a prayer that emphasizes a person's experience of God's closeness to us at every moment of our lives, no matter where we are or how we may feel:

> *Where shall I go from your Spirit?*
> *Or where shall I flee from your presence?*
> *If I ascend to heaven, you are there!*
> *If I make my bed in Sheol, you are there!*
> *If I take the wings of the morning*
> *and dwell in the uttermost parts of the sea,*
> *even there your hand will lead me,*
> *and your right hand shall hold me.*
> (Ps 139:7–10)

In our times of suffering, loneliness and near despair, a loving, caring God speaks words of tenderness and encouragement: "I made you and formed you in your mother's womb, and I will help you" (Is 44:2). As an anxious mother longs to console a suffering child, so too does God agonize with us and desire to ease our pain. The prophet Jeremiah was commanded to speak to the people for God concerning their forgetfulness of the one who loved them so deeply and wept because of their infidelity:

> *You shall say to them this word:*
> *Let my eyes run down with tears night and day,*
> *and let them not cease,*
> *for my dearly beloved people is smitten with a great wound,*
> *with a very grievous blow.*
> (Jer 14:17)

In the New Testament, it is that same affirming God who pleads with us in the words of Jesus: "Come to me, all you who labor and are burdened, and I will give you rest" (Mt 11:30).

LIKE A LOVING SHEPHERD

One of the powerful images so often used in both the Old and New Testaments to represent the affectionate, loving care of God for us is that of a shepherd. Since shepherds are not common in American society, the image needs some explanation. First of all, there is an intimate bond between a shepherd and the sheep. A shepherd knows each sheep, its unique characteristics and idiosyncrasies, and counts them often to make sure that not one has strayed from the flock. As for the sheep, they recognize and follow only the familiar voice of their shepherd. Since shepherds spend so much time alone with the sheep, they often talk to them and look upon them as companions.

The Old Testament psalmist in Psalm 23 prays to God as a shepherd and feels secure under the good shepherd's protection:

> *Even though I walk through the valley of the shadow*
> *of death,*
> *I fear no evil,*
> *for you are with me;*
> *your rod and your staff,*
> *they comfort me.*
>
> (Ps 23:4)

Through the prophet Ezekiel, God expresses grief over the neglect of the people of Israel; they were scattered over the face of the earth with no one to look after them (Ez 34:5–6). "You are my sheep," God declares to the people with tenderness, "and I am your God" (Ez 34:31). The prophet Isaiah also compares God to a shepherd who feeds the flock. Just as the shepherd takes the lambs in arm and holds them close, so does God care for us (Is 40:11).

Contrary to the false impression many people have received in church and through avenues of religious education, God does not abandon us but continues to seek us out and to draw us back again if we stray or purposely make an effort to turn against God:

> *Behold, I, I myself will search for my sheep and will seek*
> *them out. As a shepherd seeks out the flock when some of*
> *the sheep have been scattered abroad, so will I seek out my*
> *sheep. And I will rescue them from all places where they*
> *have been scattered on a day of clouds and thick darkness.*
>
> (Ez 34:11–12)

In the New Testament, Jesus applies the image of shepherd to himself. He models for us the shepherd-God of the Old Testament whose tender care for each of us is beyond our comprehension. He is the shepherd who leaves the ninety-nine in the desert and goes out to search for one lost sheep. He calls in the neighbors to rejoice when that single lost one is found (Mt 18:12–14; Lk 15:4–7).

This same shepherd will be our judge. In the gospel of Matthew, Jesus tells us that he will separate the sheep from the goats, placing the sheep on the right and the goats on the left. To those on the right, Jesus will say:

> *Come . . . inherit the kingdom prepared for you from the beginning of the world; for I was hungry and you gave me food, I was thirsty and you gave me drink, I was a stranger and you welcomed me, I was naked and you clothed me, I was sick and you visited me, I was in prison and you came to me.*
>
> (Mt 25:34–37)

Is it not consoling when we think that we are compared to sheep earlier in Matthew's gospel (18:10–14) rather than to goats? Jesus goes on to say that those on the right, the sheep, will be surprised and ask when it was that they did these things to him. And astonishing as it may seem, Jesus promises that his answer will be that when they served others with kindness in those ways, they did it to him.

In the gospel of John, Jesus refers to himself as a good and caring shepherd: "I am the good shepherd." He contrasts his care for us with that of bad shepherds who don't really take care of the sheep. Bad shepherds flee for their own lives when danger is near, and they leave the sheep alone and vulnerable to the attack of the predator. Jesus, however, assures us that his watchful loving care for us is never lacking:

> *I am the good shepherd;*
> *I know my own*
> *   and my own know me . . .*
> *I lay down my life for my sheep;*

. . . they shall never perish,
and no one shall ever snatch them out of my hand.
(Jn 10:14, 15, 28)

LIKE A CARING PHYSICIAN

A very powerful demonstration of God's care for us is shown in Jesus' deep concern for a crippled woman whom he saw, a person bent over and unable to stand erect for eighteen years (Lk 13:10–17). It was the sabbath day, and being a good observant Jew that Jesus was, many of his contemporaries would have expected him to tell her to wait and come to him the next day. Jewish respect for the sabbath was given significant importance in Israel's history more than five hundred years earlier when the Jews were in exile in Babylon. The sabbath was to be a day for praise of God and rest for all God's people, something they had taken less seriously before their exile. When it came to dealing with the pain of another person, however, Jesus' great respect for the sabbath took second place to his love for each person in spite of the reaction of other people who often stood in judgment of his actions.

Jesus could not let her wait in pain and disgrace any longer. He took the initiative and called her to him. Jesus laid his hands upon her, and she stood upright for the first time in many long years. Luke tells us that her first reaction was to praise God; that was the very purpose of the sabbath.[1]

Jesus' compassionate response to the pitiful condition of this woman, however, drew forth indignation from the synagogue leader. In order to comprehend such a negative reaction on the part of a religious official, we have to understand the logic of rabbinic interpretation of the law that forbade work on the sabbath day (Ex 20:9). First of all, Jesus did what only God had the right to do—he worked on the sabbath. The Jewish rabbis reasoned that people were born and people died on the sabbath. That meant that God worked in the giving and taking away of life on this hallowed day. Therefore, God alone could work on the sabbath; for humanity, it was a sacred day of worship and rest. Jesus' compassionate action of healing was a scandal to some people who witnessed it. As the synagogue leader perceived it, Jesus was usurping a right that belonged to God alone.

Immediately the offended Jewish synagogue official reminds the people present that there are six days on which they can be healed. They should not choose the sabbath day because healing caused the healer to work. But Jesus knows that the interpretation of the law as observed by his critics disregards the heart of the law. It makes God one who regards observance of the letter of the law more important than the human person. Moreover, how could the woman freely praise God, crippled and possessed as she was?

Jesus responds harshly to his narrow-minded critics:

> *You hypocrites! Does not each of you on the sabbath untie his ox or his ass from the manger, and lead it away to water it? Then ought not this woman, a daughter of Abraham whom Satan bound for eighteen years, be loosed from this bond on the sabbath day?*
>
> (Lk 13:15–16)

Jesus was reminding his onlookers that this woman of their own Jewish descent was of more worth than their animals. The law allowed them to untie their animals and water them on the Lord's day. The woman's lot was worse than that of animals, and without doubt she deserved far better.

Jesus took a second risk by laying his hands on the afflicted woman. According to the Pharisaic interpretation of the Mosaic law in the first century, Jesus had contaminated himself by touching an afflicted, possessed person. Good people didn't associate with others whom they considered cursed by God, because physical contact might hinder them from carrying out their rituals in praise of God. Once again Jesus put his reputation in jeopardy and ignored the false interpretation of the Jewish law, this time for the benefit of a woman who had no legal or social rights.

Freed now of the barriers that deprived her from the freedom of participating in worship and society, the woman could once more enjoy Jewish life with its social and religious opportunities. Her previous status, judged to be that of sinner and outcast and consequently reflected in her miserable condition, had been transformed into one of respect. She was free now to join in community worship and celebration.

GOD-AMONG-US IN JESUS

During desolate moments, in times of sadness and feelings of alienation from everyone, it is not unusual for a person to experience isolation and loneliness which he or she does not seek. Other people often do not know what to say, and because they feel awkward, they withdraw during the person's time of greatest need for friendship and caring concern. If a loving and understanding person who inspires trust begins to "walk beside" the distraught one as is frequently the case, the life that had become almost unbearable is gradually transformed into one that is hopeful. Suddenly and unexpectedly, the person's undisclosed and perhaps even unknown needs are met in an unsought and unusual friendship, as we see in the book *The Color Purple.*

Shug had come into Celie's life accidentally and by surprise, and they had become trusting friends. One night Celie finally got up the courage to share with Shug the shameful secret of the first incident of incest that took place when she was just a child. Celie writes in her memoirs of Shug's compassionate response. They embraced one another and cried and cried. Enfolded in her friend's arms, Celie was able to face the past and to share with Shug both the mental anguish and the physical pain she had endured. Shug gently kissed away the tears that opened the door to new life for Celie.[2]

A friend like Shug who can be trusted with another's hidden shame becomes the healing presence of Christ. Once again the injunction at Cana seems to fall on obedient ears: "Do whatever he tells you" (Jn 2:5). The friend is a gift of that seemingly unaware friend—our loving and faithful God who longs to respond to our needs and finally to celebrate as guest of our hearts.

In the story of the wedding feast of Cana, we have a powerful example of what theologians call our "salvation." However, the word "salvation" has become such a common religious term in our Judeo-Christian tradition that most of us probably miss the wealth of its meaning. As a consequence, the significance of the Cana events also remains obscured.

We owe the richness of this word to the Israelites of the Old Testament who were the first to attribute salvation to God. Before that time, the word "salvation" was used in everyday life to denote ideas such as physical rescue from harm, as well as the assurance of safety, welfare and prosperity. Since God's actions on behalf of the Israelites embodied all these aspects, they used the word to express all that God had done and would do for them in the future. "Salvation" included the notion of rescuing them from amidst the powerful and developed nations who did not know the one God. The concept also involved making them, who were poor, straggly nomads in the desert, God's very own people. The word embodied as well the concept of God's loving care and constant concern for them throughout their history.[3]

In Matthew's gospel, the concept of God's salvation as used in the Old Testament is applied to Jesus. The angel who announces his birth directs that the name "Jesus" (in Hebrew, *yeshua,* which means "savior") is to be given the child, "for he will save his people from their sins" (Mt 1:21). He will rescue them from mistaken ideas about God, and he will call all people to repent of their self-righteousness and to recognize their own sinfulness instead of focusing on that of others. They will be called to live a new life in the law of love, respect and acceptance of one another.

A wedding feast, commonly used in the Bible as a symbol of salvation, expresses God's tremendous joy in an end time celebration of final accomplishment in saving us. In Matthew's gospel, for example, Jesus compares the kingdom of heaven to a king who gave a marriage feast for his son (Mt 22:2). Everyone in the first century knew that a Jewish wedding feast generally lasted seven days. Wedding feasts were celebrations in the best sense of the word. That is why in the book of Revelation it is said that those who remain faithful to Christ unto the end are called "blessed" because they "are invited to the marriage supper of the lamb" (Rev 19:9), a symbol of joy that will never end.

The wedding feast of Cana (Jn 2:1–12), then, presents our salvation not only as a future event but as something present now in the person of Jesus. The story is a powerful example of God's fidelity and concern for us demonstrated by Jesus. The sign that Jesus worked at Cana is rich with indications of God-among-us who is sensitive to our needs and responds to them even before we are aware of them. There is no indication in the account that the bride and groom were aware of the embarrassing fact that the wine had run out. Yet when Jesus' mother calls his attention to the perplexing situation, he responds to their unconscious need. Jesus changes the water into wine so that the celebration may continue without interruption or embarrassment to the hosts.

John ends his account of Jesus' miracle by telling us that this was the first of Jesus' signs, and that it revealed the glory of Jesus (Jn 2:11). The meaning of "glory," which has its roots in the Old Testament, recalls the story of the exodus of the Jews from Egypt and their wandering in the desert. Moses told the people that they would see the "glory" of God in the morning. He was referring to the saving gift of manna that God would send to satisfy their hunger (Ex 16:7–10).[4] That miracle in the desert was a striking action on the part of God that revealed God-among-us—a loving, caring, and compassionate God.

At the wedding feast of Cana in the New Testament, we see God-among-us demonstrating that same caring concern that God lavished upon the people of the Old Testament. In the two chapters that follow in John's gospel, one of the dominant themes is the replacement by Jesus of the traditional Jewish rituals and institutions which were thought to be one's insurance to gaining salvation and access to God. The ritual cleansings and temple sacrifices lost their meaning once God came to live among us in Jesus. The way to God became Jesus himself as Jesus explained to Thomas: "I am the way . . ." (Jn 14:5).

The waters in the jars at the wedding feast (Jn 2:6) were probably used for Jewish purification rituals connected with such feasts. Jesus had them filled and he changed these waters into the best of wines. He thereby shows that before God became human and one of us, the old institutions were good in their purpose and origins. Now, however, Jesus replaces them, and he himself becomes the most perfect and sure way to God.

The wedding feast of Cana, therefore, is the celebration of God-among-us in the person of Jesus. Not even worship or ritual in the ornate temple of Jerusalem was enough to satisfy God's desire for relationship with all of humanity. The temple, in fact, had become a source of division between "the righteous" and "sinners," because it allowed access to God only to those who were ritually clean. Nothing less than God becoming a human being and living among us (Jn 1:14) could demonstrate God's care for us and desire for nearness to us.

The prophet Hosea spoke of God's wish to have a mutual and loving relationship with us. When the people of the northern kingdom (often referred to as "Ephraim" in the Old Testament) were turning to other gods, God yearned with nostalgia for the days when their early relationship was as tender as that between a loving adult and a toddler:

> *It was I who taught Ephraim to walk,*
> *I took them up in my arms;*
> *but they did not know that it was I who healed them.*
> *I led them with cords of compassion,*
> *with the bands of love.*
> *I became to them as one*
> *who eases the yoke on their jaws.*
> *I bent down to them and fed them gently.*
>
> (Hos 11:3–4)

In the gospel of John, Jesus uses an allegory to express the intimate relationship he has with us: "I am the vine; you are the branches" (Jn 15:5). One of the saddest lines in all of scripture appears in the first chapter of that same gospel. In speaking of Jesus as the "Word," or the human expression of God come to live in our midst as one of us, we hear the sad lament:

> *He was in the world,*
> *and the world was made through him,*
> *yet the world knew him not.*
> *He came to his own home,*
> *and his own people received him not.*
>
> (Jn 1:10–11)

Jesus knew well the experience of rejection and the pain that accompanies the human condition. Paul, in his letter to the Philippians, states it well:

> *Though he was in the form of God,*
> *he did not count equality with God*
> *a thing to be grasped,*
> *but emptied himself,*

taking the form of a servant,
being born in the likeness of humanity.
(Phil 2:6–7)

As a human person, Christ endured all that any one of us might have to go through—joy, sorrow, pain, suffering, etc.

The gospels speak of Jesus' care and concern for people who were suffering as having "compassion" on them. "Compassion" in Greek expresses a deep-down "gut" reaction to something sad. Luke, for example, uses "compassion" in his gospel to speak of Jesus' response to the poor widow whom he saw accompanying her dead son in a funeral procession (Lk 7:11–15). The boy was her only son and therefore his mother's breadwinner. The poor widow would have no one to look after her needs.

The widow asked Jesus for nothing; in fact, there is no indication that she recognized Jesus' presence, nor that she knew anything about him. But that made no difference to one who was touched so deeply and saddened by the sight. Jesus took the initiative, touched the bier, and stopped the funeral procession. He was not concerned that he had made himself ritually unclean by coming into physical contact with the pall on which the dead man lay. Jesus cared more about the suffering woman than he did about the law. He raised the young man to life and "gave him to his mother" (Lk 7:15).

When sorrow weighs us down, Jesus is also present with us, wishing to be our strength. Like the psalmist who cries out to God, we can cry out to Jesus who is God-among-us, loving and caring for us:

Be a rock of refuge for me,
a strong fortress to save me.
(Ps 31:2)

JESUS PROMISES TO CONTINUE HIS CARE FOR US

In the last supper scene in the gospel of John, Jesus speaks with a note of sadness about leaving his disciples. He knows how much they have come to love him and how much they will miss his physical presence among them. But Jesus has a plan: "I will not leave you orphans; I will come to you" (Jn 14:18). He promises to do this by sending them the Holy Spirit whom he calls the "Paraclete." Since "Paraclete" is not a word common to our English language, many translations render the Greek word *parakletos* as "Counselor," "Advocate," "Consoler," or simply as "Holy Spirit."

To capture the richness of the gift of the Paraclete that Jesus promised, it is necessary to understand the various nuances of the Greek word *parakletos*. They refer to specific roles that Jesus filled in relation to us when he was still on earth and which are continued in the gift of the Spirit or Paraclete.

One aspect of Jesus' relationship to us which is perpetuated by the Paraclete was that of teacher. Jesus promised that his teaching which came from God would not cease when he was gone from this earth:

> *But the Paraclete, the Holy Spirit,*
> *whom the Father will send in my name,*
> *will teach you all things,*
> *and bring to your remembrance*
> *all that I have said to you.*
>
> (Jn 14:26)

Jesus recognizes the heaviness of heart that the disciples are experiencing at the thought of his leaving them:

> *I have many things to say to you,*
> *but you cannot bear them now.*
> *When the Spirit of truth comes,*
> *he will guide you in all truth;*
> *for he will not speak on his own authority,*
> *but whatever he hears he will speak. . . .*
> *He will glorify me,*
> *for he will take what is mine*
> *and declare it to you.*
>
> (Jn 16:12–14)

Sensitive teacher that Jesus is, he now teaches us through the Paraclete or Holy Spirit who lives in us.

Another aspect of Jesus' relationship to us was that of consoler. He was present to those who were completely excluded from society and religion or relegated to the fringes. For many people of Jesus' day, he was the only person who showed them disinterested care and concern. In his great love for us, Jesus assures us in the fourth gospel that this consolation will not cease:

> *Now I am going to the one who sent me. . . .*
> *But because I have said these things to you,*
> *sorrow has filled your hearts.*
> *Nevertheless, I tell you the truth:*
> *it is to your advantage that I go away*
> *for if I do not go away,*
> *the Paraclete will not come to you.*
>
> (Jn 16:5–7)

Now the Paraclete plays the role of Jesus who was our consoler. No longer will Jesus walk among us; he will live in us in the Holy Spirit as the guest of our hearts, teaching, consoling and being the presence of Jesus with us.

Jesus was also the defender of the downtrodden, the sick, and those in need. The Paraclete now carries out that role. In classical Greek, long before the New Testament writings appeared, the word "paraclete" was used in a legal sense to refer to a defense attorney.[5] The literal meaning of the Greek word is "one called alongside." The role of a defense attorney is to stand by a person in trouble, to be an advocate for her or him. Some translations render the Greek word as "advocate" to convey this aspect of its meaning. When John wrote the fourth gospel, members of his church community were being dragged before synagogues, harassed and punished because of their insistence that Jesus was indeed the Son of God and messiah king whom they had long awaited in their history. Today our historical situation has changed. Few people in the world have to suffer physically for their faith in Jesus. Yet, as we face the difficulties of living out the values Jesus taught us in a world that ignores those values and is often hostile to people who practice them, we still need a defender to stand by us and help us in troubled times.

In order to fully appreciate the gift that is ours in the Holy Spirit, we need to understand all the nuances of meanings for the word *parakletos*. They help us recall that Jesus is still our teacher, our consoler, and our advocate. He continues his care for us as he promised in his prayer at the final meal with his disciples:

> *I am praying for them . . .*
> *whom you have given me,*
> *for they are yours . . .*
> *all mine are yours,*
> *and yours are mine.*
> (Jn 17:9–10)

With Jesus' death and resurrection, we are not abandoned as orphans with no one to care for us, nor as sheep left to the wolves. Jesus remains not only with us but in us in the Paraclete, still loving and living out the assurance of God in the Old Testament:

> *I have loved you with an everlasting love;*
> *therefore I have continued my faithfulness to you.*
> (Jer 31:3)

V

God Is Faithful in Consoling Us

❖   ❖   ❖

For you shall go out in joy,
   and be led forth in peace;
the mountains and the hills before you
   shall break forth in singing,
   and all the trees of the field shall clap their hands.

(Is 55:12)

Through years of bearing silently a burden of guilt and shame, many people gradually transfer a more mature understanding of a situation to circumstances which occurred much earlier in life. They fail to realize that in actuality there was little or no objective comprehension of what was happening to them or around them at that time. As a result, they now view themselves as deceptive and unworthy of trust and love.

Many adult children of alcoholic parents and divorcees think that something they consciously or unconsciously did caused the tragedy that caused family division and pain. They suffer untold agony over a situation which was entirely beyond their control. Other persons who were sexually molested as children continue to suffer secretly as adults and often blame themselves. They tend to think that perhaps if they had not acted in a particular manner, "it" might never have happened. Repeatedly they ponder past events and wish in vain that they could change them all.

The personal worlds of many of these people have been blown to smithereens. Their lives have been devastated to the extent that they cannot envision its broken pieces ever again being pieced back together. One woman expressed her pain metaphorically as "a shattered cup, the pieces of which can never be put together again."

Where is God when such feelings begin to haunt these sincere persons? In Jesus we see the authentic God who experiences our pain and weeps with us. He endured rejection and even death because of his message of God's mercy and love for every person. When the present appears to exclude all possibilities of comfort, Jesus consoles us with the promise of a time in the future when suffering will be no more.

The promise of such a future is found in the book of Revelation which was written for a desperate community of the late first century who suffered deprivations and persecution because of their choice of Christianity. It seemed that there could be no remedy for so cruel a world, one that opposed, rejected and caused them physical, social and financial hardships and suffering.

The author of the book of Revelation describes in symbolic language an ideal future for his suffering people. This future of perfection, happiness and peace still offers hope to Christians in painful situations where faith and trust are sorely tried:

> *Then I saw a new heaven and a new earth; for the first heaven and the first earth had passed away, and the sea was no more. And I saw the holy city, new Jerusalem, coming down out of heaven from God, prepared as a bride adorned for her husband; and I heard a loud voice from the throne saying, "Behold, the dwelling of God with humanity. In dwelling with them, they shall be God's own people, and God will be with them, wiping away every tear from their eyes. Death shall be no more; neither shall there be mourning nor crying nor pain, for the former things have passed away." And God . . . said, "Behold, I make all things new. . . . To the thirsty I will give from the fountain of the water of life without payment."*
>
> (Rev 21:1–6)

In the future creation described in Revelation, all the negative things of this world (symbolized by the sea) will disappear: ". . . and the sea was no more." To the people of the ancient world the sea was considered evil, a dwelling place of diabolic forces and hideous monsters. The powerful sea seemed to be the enemy of humanity since it appeared to the unscientific eye that it swallowed up people and ships alike. In the description of the new creation there could be nothing evil; a sea, therefore, served as a perfect symbol for that which was not good.

The promise of an end to evil and everything being made new is comforting to persons looking for a thread of hope which would signal the end to suffering and pain. But must they wait until some distant future for an alleviation of suffering? In the new creation described in Revelation, it is God living in the midst of the people that makes it ideal. It is the God that Jesus modeled for us—a God who shares our sadness, who empathizes when we hurt, a God who consoles even the lowliest of persons. We have that God with us now in Jesus who wants to soothe our pain and protect us from further heartache. It is the same God of the Old Testament who asked:

> *Can a mother forget her infant,*
> *be without tenderness for the child of her womb?*
> *Even should she forget,*
> *I will never forget you.*
>
> (Is 49:15)

A woman who has experienced pregnancy knows well the preoccupation of a mother with her unborn child. To forget it would be unthinkable, and so it is with God in relationship to each of us. Each individual is special to God, and not one of us is ever forgotten, even for a moment.

GOD SEARCHES OUT THE ALIENATED

In the gospel of Matthew, Jesus claims that not even an insignificant sparrow goes without God's attention, and that we are of far more value than little birds (Mt 10:29–30). Many of the parables or stories Jesus told express this loving concern of God for us. The parables of the lost sheep and the lost coin offer consolation to those who feel that their past life experiences leave no hope for them in relation to God and even less to significant others.

The parable of the lost sheep in Luke 15:4–7 is prefaced by the murmuring of some religious leaders. In their self-proclaimed righteousness, they resent the fact that Jesus ignores their time-held social custom of alienating so-called "sinners" and "outcasts." The parable not only illustrates the concern that each person realize his or her worth in the eyes of God, but it also shows an understanding of each one's need to feel a part of a community or a group.

Jesus tells us of a God far different from the image which the scribes and Pharisees endorsed. Jesus concentrates on the joy of God over one who has been "lost," rather than on what the "lost" one has done. In the parable of the lost sheep he stresses the anxious activity of God when one of us is lost. Jesus asks his critics:

> *Which one of you, having a hundred sheep, if he has lost one of them does not leave the ninety-nine in the desert, and go after the one which is lost, until he finds it? And when he has found it, he lays it on his shoulders, rejoicing. And when he comes home, he calls together his friends and his neighbors, saying to them, "Rejoice with me, for I have found my sheep which was lost." Just so, I tell you, there will be more joy in heaven over one sinner who repents than over ninety-nine righteous persons who need no repentance.*
>
> (Lk 15:4–7)

One's initial reaction may be empathy for the ninety-nine who remained faithful and did not stray. As a consequence of their fidelity, they are left in the desert while the shepherd goes looking for one that did not stay with the flock but carelessly wandered off alone. Would it not be better to be the lost one who is given all the attention?

To understand this parable, we have to examine the rest of the gospel for the way Luke uses "desert" (*eremos* in Greek). In every circumstance, it is a place of solitude and communication with God. The austere John the Baptist lived a secluded life of prayer and self-abnegation in the desert until he began his public preaching of repentance in preparation for the coming of God's reign (Lk 1:80). Jesus, at the beginning of his ministry, was led by the Spirit into the desert, and though he was tested by the devil there, it was a place of his triumph over Satan (Lk 4:1–13). Throughout his life Jesus is said to have withdrawn to the "desert" to pray: "And when it was day, he departed and went into a lonely place (*eremos*)" (Lk 4:42); "He withdrew to the wilderness (*eremos*) and prayed" (Lk 5:16); "And he took them and went aside privately into a desert place (*eremos*) . . ." (Lk 9:10).

From Luke's use of the word "desert," we may conclude that the shepherd does not neglect the ninety-nine faithful ones. To the contrary, they are left in a place of solitude and communication with God. Moreover, they are together as a flock, and because of that the dangers of the "desert" are less hazardous. This interpretation is borne out by the importance Luke places on community in his other writing, the Acts of the Apostles. There we find the early followers of Jesus sticking together as a community in the midst of danger of persecution after Jesus' death and resurrection.

The aspect that Luke emphasizes is that for Jesus, the lost one has withdrawn from God, but God will never withdraw from the person. Instead, the "lost" one is searched for, and when found, God shoulders him or her and calls a celebration. As the psalmist articulates so well, "Yahweh lifts up those who are bowed down" (Ps 146:9).

God is portrayed in the same light in the parable of the lost coin that follows the parable of the lost sheep in Luke 15:8–10. A woman who has lost a coin lights a lamp and searches for it until she finds it. She then calls her friends and neighbors to rejoice with her. So it is with God when one of us is lost. God also "lights a lamp," as it were, to illumine the darkness into which we have plunged ourselves.

Again, as in the parable of the lost sheep, the activity of searching and rejoicing at the success of the search occurs at the initiative of God. God's love does not cease when we break communication, and neither does God wait for us to take the first step back. The God whom Jesus taught about never gives up on us and never stops loving us and looking for us no matter how long we may persevere in turning our backs.

Nevertheless, God does not curtail our freedom, but gives us room to make mistakes as in the case of Israel in the Old Testament:

> *Like an eagle that stirs up its nest,*
> *that flutters over its young,*
> *spreading out its wings, catching them,*
> *bearing them on its pinions,*
> *Yahweh alone did lead them.*
> (Dt 32:11)

Like a mother eagle, God lets us "try our wings," even if it involves a search for complete independence in our quest for fulfillment. But when our "wings" prove too weak and our self-confidence degenerates into failure, our God is there like a mother eagle waiting and ready to bear us up and bring us back to safety if we but allow it.

GOD REMEMBERS ONLY OUR GOODNESS

What a consolation to hear from Jesus that God does not concentrate on our sinfulness but rather focuses on the goodness that is the reality of each of us! Jesus told a parable to depict this almost unbelievable aspect of God's love for us. In Luke 15:11–32, Jesus compared God to an ideal parent. He told a parable of a man who had two sons. The younger son was probably a teenager since the word in Greek (*neoteros*) in other places in the New Testament usually refers to an unmarried man. The age for marriage in the Jewish culture of the first century was about eighteen.

The younger son in the parable decided to leave home and boldly asked his father for his share of the inheritance. The father granted his wish and divided his property between him and his older brother. The younger son cashed in his share and set out for a distant country. His adventures led him to an immoral life in which he recklessly spent all his inheritance and eventually found himself reduced to poverty and want.

So low had the young Jewish man fallen that he went to work for a Gentile who had pigs. Jewish law stated that feeding swine made a person unclean (Lev 11:7), but the desperate and famished youngster nevertheless took up the dreaded occupation. He had degraded himself about as much as a Jew of that time possibly could. Now penniless and disgraced, the young man's friends on whom he had squandered his money were no longer around. So hungry was he that he would gladly have eaten the food that the pigs were given.

The youth's misery, however, proved to be a saving experience for him. In his degradation he remembered how good he had had it at home. Even the servants in his father's house were faring better than he. The wretched boy realized that in all fairness he had no right to return home as a dependent son, but he decided to go back anyway and ask to be a slave there.

> *He would say to his father: "Father, I have sinned against heaven and against you; I am no longer worthy to be called your son; treat me as one of your hired servants." And he arose and came to his father. But while he was yet at a distance his father saw him and had compassion, and ran and embraced him and kissed him. And the son said to him, "Father, I have sinned against heaven and before you; I am no longer worthy to be called your son." But the father said to the servants, "Bring quickly the best robe, and put it on him; and put a ring on his hand, and shoes on his feet; and bring the fatted calf and kill it, and let us eat and make merry; for this son of mine was dead, and is alive again; he was lost and is found." And they began to make merry.*
> (Lk 15:18–23)

Notice that the renegade son was first motivated by selfishness to return home; he needed food for his hungry stomach. He did say in his mind that he would admit his guilt to his father. In the story, however, repentance is not indicated as the primary motive in his decision to return home.

The father's response is totally selfless. When he sees his estranged son in the distance, he is filled with compassion, a word in Greek which implies a gut-level feeling that comes from deep within a person. There is no indication whatsoever that the son had bathed or become legally clean according to Jewish prescriptions of law. Yet the father is not deterred by such preoccupations. He runs to meet his wayward son and greets him with hugs and kisses.

The young man begins to confess his guilt, but the father interrupts before his son can even suggest that he might be taken back as a slave in his former home. The wise father knows that his servitude would be a constant reminder of his past sinful life, not only to the young man himself, but to all who saw him. He does not want that kind of life for his son. The father wants instead to focus on the present; his son's past is of no interest to him. He therefore demands that "the best robe," a symbol of dignity and respect, be put on his son. He orders that a ring be put on his finger. The ring to which he refers is probably the signet ring used only by one in authority to imprint the official seal on important documents. The father is indicating that his son will be given not only a place of honor in his home, but also one of authority. Moreover, he commands that they put shoes on his feet, the trademark of a free person in contrast to a barefooted slave. For this loving father, there would be no looking back. His son had profited from his mistakes, and his return was reason for great rejoicing. The past was to be forgotten.

The parable continues with the older son's angry reaction when he hears of the joyful celebration for the younger spendthrift who had wasted his father's earnings and had lived with harlots. Enraged, the older brother refuses to enter the house from which echoed merriment, music and dance. Again the loving father takes the initiative with this recalcitrant son, the one who had always remained faithful and at home with him. He goes outside where his envious son sulks alone and talks with him. The elder brother complains bitterly that there had never been a fatted calf killed in celebration of his fidelity to his father.

Unlike his father, this older son wishes to focus only on the sinfulness of the one to whom he refers as "this son of yours" rather than as "my brother." Nevertheless, the patient and understanding father responds in loving kindness. He concentrates on the good that he perceives in his resentful son:

> *Son, you are always with me and all that is mine is yours. It was fitting to make merry and be glad, for this your brother was dead, and is alive; he was lost, and is found.*
>
> (Lk 15:31–32)

There is no scolding for his jealous son's behavior, only reassurance and an explanation for the joy of the celebration for his younger son.

Jesus shows us in this parable that God also regards our past in like manner. There is no need to beat ourselves for a former way of life that in no way can we undo. The present is ours to live, and the future lies before us with a loving, forgiving and consoling God to accompany us.

STRENGTH IN WEAKNESS

Human weakness is often a tremendous source of discouragement. If, however, we look at the persons chosen by God to do important tasks in the history of our salvation, we may be consoled. The roster is far from being a list of virtuous and honorable people.

Old Testament writers did not hide the weaknesses of their heroes and heroines. We find shocking stories about the behavior of some of the persons Matthew listed in the genealogy, the ancestral line of Jesus in his gospel (Mt 1:2–26).

If we judge by human standards, we might conclude that God was a poor personnel manager. To begin with, God chooses a wretched nomadic people, uneducated and with no written language at that time, to be the ancestor of a race that was to bring forth a savior. The Babylonians, the contemporaries of the ancient Hebrews, were already a literate and developed nation. Yet God did not choose the strong and efficient.

Some of the stories of individual characters found in the Old Testament and named in the genealogy of Jesus leave one no less dubious. Abraham, the first great ancestor, lied to the king of Gerar and said that Sarah was only his sister when in fact she was his wife (Gen 20). Rebekah succeeded in convincing her son Jacob to cheat his brother Esau out of his birthright by deceiving his blind father and pretending that he was Esau (Gen 27). Judah had intercourse with his daughter-in-law who posed as a harlot to him (Gen 39). Rahab, another woman Matthew includes in the genealogy, was a harlot by trade (Jos 2). David, the greatest of Israel's kings, lusted after Bathsheba and had her husband placed on the front line during a fierce battle so that he would be killed and David could have Bathsheba for himself (2 Sam 11). Solomon, remembered mostly for his wisdom, became so greedy for luxury and fame that he oppressed the northern people of his kingdom by demanding unjust taxation to support his projects and affluent life style. His excessive debauchery is described in terms of having seven hundred wives who turned his heart to other gods, in addition to princesses and three hundred concubines (1 Kgs 9–11). The kings that follow in Matthew's genealogy fail to improve the picture. The account of each one's reign in the first book of Kings generally ends with a statement that the king did what was evil in God's sight.

Human weakness is clearly not an obstacle to God's activity on our behalf. Paul, to whom the risen Lord gave the task of evangelizing the Gentiles, says that he prayed to be delivered from weakness. In view of the weaknesses of Jesus' ancestral line, God's answer to Paul's prayer is not surprising: "My grace is sufficient for you, for my power is made perfect in weakness" (2 Cor 12:9). Paul goes on to claim that he is content with weakness, "for when I am weak, then I am strong" (2 Cor 12:10). This is not to say that the apostle gave up the struggle to overcome his weaknesses. His prayer indicates his detachment from self-reliance and a total dependence on God's grace. Only when we face our weakness and humbly acknowledge our reliance on God can God work unimpeded in us and through us. This realization is encouraging to a person who is on the brink of giving up in the face of human frailty.

A QUIET PRESENCE IN STORMY MOMENTS

In the course of life's experiences, most of us have learned that what we know with our heads is not always supported by our feelings and emotions. For some persons, the ghost of a past with its burden of guilt seems to rear up its head and come suddenly and vividly alive and real as if it were the present at that moment. Old wounds begin to open, and fears which they had thought were long put to rest surge up anew.

Luke's story of the storm on the lake in Galilee (Lk 8:22–25) presents a consoling picture of frightened disciples with whom one might easily relate in moments of fear. The narrative differs from Mark's account in several ways (see Mk 4:35–41), but what is most important for our attention is the added emphasis in the Lukan story. Not only is Jesus shown to be one who has power over the waves in a storm as in Mark's gospel, but his power reveals his compassion for those who suffer fear as well as his willingness to do something to help them.

Luke tells us that one day the disciples and Jesus got into a boat and were crossing the lake, and on the way across, Jesus fell asleep. As is common on the lake, a sudden storm arose, caused by a wind funneled down the steep mountains that surround the lake. The disciples were naturally frightened, for their lives were in danger. They awakened Jesus with the despairing announcement that they were perishing.

> *And he awoke and rebuked the wind and raging waves; and they ceased and they were calm. He said to them, "Where is your faith?"*
>
> (Lk 8:24–25)

Luke goes on to say that the disciples were filled with fear and wonder at Jesus' power over the wind and the waters.

Jesus does not suggest that the disciples lack faith as he does in Mark's account. Rather, the implication in Luke's version of the incident is that they actually *are* persons of faith. Their faith, however, becomes weak on occasion and fails to sustain their trust in the power of God as shown in Jesus.

When moments of fear over one's past suddenly rise up like giant waves that are capable of drowning the person, and fill him or her with overwhelming anxiety, the episode on the lake is consoling. There is one to whom we can always cry out as did the disciples in the boat: "Lord, we are perishing!" That fearful cry is no indication that one lacks faith, but it does show that the anxiety experienced seems to obscure a deep faith in Jesus. Such moments are certainly not reasons to fill one with shame. They might instead serve as occasions to be grateful that one recognizes and acknowledges the fear rather than ignoring or pretending that it does not exist. Such times can be moments of grace when dependence on God is reinforced. God may seem to be entirely unconcerned and unaware, but, as in Luke's story, Jesus has unmasked for us a God who is always there, desiring to save us from being overpowered.

Little by little the process of healing will bring a time of rejoicing. Then we will be able to cry out wholeheartedly with the psalm writer who speaks of tense days already past when Jerusalem was in danger of siege from its powerful enemies:

> *When God delivered Zion from bondage,*
> *   it seemed like a dream.*
> *Then was our mouth filled with laughter,*
> *   on our lips there were songs.*
> (Ps 126:1–2)

VI

God Calls Us to Personal Growth

❖   ❖   ❖

I call you by your name,
. . . though you do not know me.
I am the Lord, and there is no other.
                                        (Is 45:4)

The last chapters dealt mainly with biblical texts that emphasize a faithful, loving, forgiving, caring and consoling God. They stressed that regardless of our response, God never changes but loves and accepts us as we are in the growth process of life's journey.

Acceptance, however, does not exclude the fact that God summons us to personal growth as a result of pain and misfortune. To grovel in the misery of the past is to close our eyes to the grandeur, uniqueness and potential that are ours precisely because of each person's singular life experiences.

Our call to growth and wholeness has its beginnings with the ancient Israelites. The prophet Hosea expressed God's call as teaching the people to walk and as leading them with the cords of compassion (Hos 12:3–4). Throughout the Old Testament, there is evidence of a slow but gradual coming to understand God's love and their vocation to a mutual love relationship as the essence of happiness and wholeness.

The people of the Old Testament often tended to transfer their own human modes of action to God as we sometimes do. Hence we find the primitive idea that their God hated those whom the Israelites hated, or that God was angry and revengeful when they themselves sinned. Unfortunately, the misunderstanding of this process of Israel's coming to know their God better and the transferal of their own human reactions to God has led many sincere people to reject the Old Testament. These ancient writings, however, provide insight into the God who created us out of love and beckons each of us to move forward to personal growth. They help us to comprehend that God understands the depths of our pain as we make the journey, as well as our need for space and time to grow. The Old Testament writings also demonstrate that God, as a loving parent, can handle our anger and feelings of revenge as we experience our growing pains. Furthermore, they challenge us with the message that this divine healer and instructor desires to teach us to walk steadily, to love ourselves as we are, and not to flounder hopelessly in past negative experiences.

INVITATION TO LIGHT

Sometimes a person's history has been so crippling to one's personality or reputation that other people lose faith in the ability of the struggling individual to get up and go forward again. The person is hindered in efforts to pick up the pieces and begin life anew, not only by others' lack of trust, but also by some people's overt rejection and determination to make the past a stumbling block.

God, however, never gives up on us or blocks the way we choose to progress. Even if the path chosen is unwise, our freedom will be respected. God will accompany us on the perilous journey, be present to us when the darkness threatens to overwhelm us, and gently lead us to follow the way to genuine happiness.

In Mark's gospel, Jesus models for us the authentic God who has compassion on those who suffer and who calls each of us from darkness to a more human and free life. Mark tells us the story of the blind beggar Bartimaeus who was sitting by the roadside and crying out to Jesus as he passed. Since many people of Jesus' time looked upon physical disabilities and sicknesses as a sign of God's disfavor, those around Bartimaeus tried desperately to silence him. The writer comments that the people surrounding him "rebuked" him, a word which is often used in Mark's gospel in reference to evil spirits. "But he cried out all the more: 'Jesus, Son of David, have mercy on me'" (Mk 10:47).

When Bartimaeus asked for "mercy," he was asking for something that surpasses pity or compassion. "Mercy" in the biblical sense involves a mutual relationship between God and us, a relationship of love, loyalty, forgiveness, compassion and trust. Even though we may fail in our fidelity to God, we can still expect "mercy" from God whose relationship with us is freely chosen and not subject to our changing whims.

Bartimaeus' cry, "Son of David," gave recognition to the role of Jesus as king. Since Bartimaeus was a beggar and blind, the reaction of the people around Bartimaeus is not surprising. How could a person who was cursed by God recognize who was, or who was not, the long awaited messiah of Israel? Surely only the just and learned could discern a matter of such sacred importance in their history. Moreover, if Jesus was indeed the long awaited king from the ancestral line of their great King David, a person of Bartimaeus' status had no right to address him.

Bartimaeus, however, had voiced the true meaning of Jesus' kingship. As with the original notion of king in the ancient world (one who sat at the city gates and was advocate for the poor and the powerless), Jesus responds likewise to this blind wretch of first century society. "Call him," Jesus commanded (Mk 10:49). Immediately, Bartimaeus cast away his mantle or outer cloak, a garment worn by day and used as a cover at night. He jumped up and went to Jesus.

> *Jesus asked the man, "What do you want me to do for you?"*
> *And the blind man said to him, "Master, let me receive my*
> *sight." And Jesus said to him, "Go your way; your faith has*
> *made you well." And immediately he received his sight and*
> *followed him on the way.*
>
> (Mk 10:51–52)

Bartimaeus refused to be imprisoned behind the walls of society's expectations of his place in life. He recognized the opportunity that was his at the moment, and, trusting God's faithfulness, he cried out to Jesus for help. In turn Jesus called Bartimaeus out of the darkness of his blindness into the light. By casting aside his cloak, Bartimaeus symbolically gave up his security and relied totally on Jesus. He followed Jesus "on the way." "The way" in Mark's gospel is the way to Jerusalem, the place of crucifixion and resurrection. It is also a symbol of the path of discipleship, that of the cross, for anyone who responds to the call of Jesus.

Each time a person accepts the call of Jesus to move forward with him on life's journey to wholeness, the past with its false securities becomes secondary. Like Bartimaeus who cast aside his cloak of security, one's values change. Not even the taunting voices of those who criticize and try to keep the person in place will be effective any longer.

Following the call of Jesus to wholeness is never easy. In Matthew's gospel, Jesus expresses his way as one of total insecurity: "The foxes have holes, and birds of the air have nests; but the Son of man has nowhere to lay his head" (Mt 8:20).

A CALL TO FIDELITY

Periods of weakness and alienation from God can be compared to Israel's time of exile in Babylon (587–538 B.C.E.). In Isaiah 58 God invites Israel to return. The things Israel needs are waiting to be given freely by God and without a "bill" to be paid. They cannot be earned or bought by good deeds, prayers or promises. God's desire for Israel's return is so intense that nothing is required except detachment from evil ways and thoughts:

> *Lo, all who thirst,*
> *come to the waters.*
> *And they who have no money,*
> *come, buy and eat.*
> *Come, buy wine and milk*
> *without money and without price. . . .*
> *Let the wicked forsake their ways,*
> *and the righteous their thoughts.*
> *Let them return . . .*
> *for God will abundantly pardon.*
> *For my thoughts are not your thoughts,*
> *neither are your ways my ways.*
> (Is 55:1, 7–8)

One might object: "The 'catch 22,' however, is that I can't give up my sinfulness." God has never asked that we justify ourselves. In fact, in the Old Testament the prophet Zephaniah assures Israel that God, not Israel, has done the work:

> *Yahweh has taken away the judgments against you,*
>   *and cast out your enemies. . . .*
> *You shall fear evil no more. . . .*
> *God is in your midst,*
>   *a warrior who gives victory.*
>   (Zeph 3:15–17)

It was clearly not Israel's strength that brought deliverance, but rather God's work on Israel's behalf.

In the New Testament, Paul expresses the same notion when he states that we all have sinned and are justified, or made righteous, by God's grace as gift through Jesus Christ (Rom 3:24). When Paul speaks of "justice" or "righteousness," he is using the word in its Hebrew sense. Among the people of the ancient Mediterranean world, any person who was faithful in keeping promises made to another was referred to as being *sadeq,* a word translated into English as "just" or "righteous." When the Israelites wanted to speak of God's faithfulness in keeping promises made to them, they used the same word, *sadeq,* or "just." The word had nothing to do with the idea that God gives us what we deserve—punishment for bad deeds, reward for the good we do. The latter meaning is a Roman notion of justice. Even though Paul had Roman citizenship, he was thoroughly Jewish in his mode of thinking. To put it in his own words, "I was advanced in Judaism beyond many of my own age among my people, so extremely zealous was I for the traditions of my ancestors" (Gal 1:14).

Paul's notion of God's justifying us is his expression of the Old Testament idea of justification; through Jesus Christ, God makes us capable of being faithful. Left to ourselves, we would be helpless in the face of sin. Christ, however, becomes our strength, our fidelity to God, so that we in turn might become the faithfulness of God in our day-to-day lives:

*For our sake God made him [Christ] to be sin, who knew no
sin, so that in him we might become the righteousness
of God.*

(2 Cor 5:21)

Paul emphasizes our inability to be faithful by our own strength
in his assertion that we are justified by grace as a gift. That gift is given
us "by faith apart from works" (Rom 3:28). Again, Paul is using the
Hebrew sense of the word "faith." He is not speaking of an intellec-
tual exercise; he is referring to a total reliance upon God. Like the
prophet Zephaniah, who reminded Israel that their return was not
earned, but was instead God's gift, so also Paul stresses in the letter to
the Romans that as human beings we cannot give up our sinfulness by
the power of our own strength. Our victory over sin is God's work in
us through Jesus Christ. All we can do is to be humbly open to the gift
of fidelity that God offers and rely totally upon Christ to be faithful in
accomplishing that gift in us:

*God gives power to the faint,
and to the one who has no might God increases strength.*

(Is 40:29)

Epilogue

❖   ❖   ❖

Insight into God's fidelity to us affects our whole lives. Integration of the realization of a loving and faithful God makes prayer, for example, freer and more spontaneous. Though prayer is sometimes formal, it need not always be so. Basically, prayer is a mutual communication with God who is our constant companion, one to whom we can pour out our heart's love and joy, fears and regrets, desires and hopes, and to whom we listen in turn. God's response comes in various and unexpected ways—in the events of our lives, the people we meet, the beauty of nature, the counsel of wise persons, the words of scripture, or through quiet, peaceful reflection.

When we trust that God will remain faithful, we are free to express whatever emotions overflow from our hearts. In our moments of desolation, we can cry out as Jesus did in his feelings of abandonment in Mark's account of Jesus' agony on the cross: "My God, my God, why have you forsaken me?" (Mk 15:34). When our faith in God's fidelity wavers, words such as those of the parent who wanted Jesus to cure his son may be all that we can muster: "I believe. Help my unbelief" (Mk 9:24). The reproach of the frightened disciples in the storm-tossed boat, "Teacher, do you not care if we perish?" (Mk 4:38), exemplifies the freedom of persons who feel secure in their relationship with Jesus.

The psalms of the Old Testament may become more meaningful than ever before in life, as ancient prayers that express every emotion of the human heart: "Give thanks to the Lord who is good" (Ps 106:1); "I am weary with my moaning; every night I flood my bed with tears" (Ps 6:6); "O Lord, be not far from me" (Ps 35:22); "Draw the spear and the javelin against my pursuers" (Ps 35:3); "For God alone my soul waits in silence" (Ps 62:1); "O God, you know my folly; the wrongs I have done are not hidden from you" (Ps 69:5).

The book of Jonah in the Old Testament is a fascinating and comical tale which portrays a God who is "merciful, slow to anger, and abounding in steadfast love" (Jon 4:2). At the same time it is a good illustration of the freedom and spontaneity that we as human beings can have in our conversations with God. Jonah's desire to see the Gentile Ninevites destroyed, his initial refusal to preach repentance to them, and God's final success in getting him to do so ends in a conversation between God and Jonah. Jonah is angry that the plant which God caused to spring up to protect him from the sun had withered while Jonah waited to see what would happen to the city:

> But God said to Jonah, "Do you do well to be angry for the plant?" And he said, "I do well to be angry, angry enough to die." And the Lord said, "You pity the plant, for which you did not labor, nor did you make it grow, which came into being in a night, and perished in a night. And should not I pity Nineveh, that great city, in which there are more than a hundred and twenty thousand persons who do not know their right hand from their left, and also much cattle?"
> (Jon 4:9–11)

Self-confidence is another area of a person's life which is greatly affected by the conviction of God's unconditional love for us. In John's gospel, there is a marvelous story in which a man blind from birth is transformed from a beggar to a challenger of religious authorities (Jn 9:1–41). The narrative demonstrates on the one hand the spiritual blindness of people who think they see or know who Jesus is and thus refuse to accept the truth when presented with it. On the other hand, the physical blindness of a man is turned not only to sight but to spiritual insight about Jesus, a truth which he bravely defends.

The man, considered by those who saw him to be a sinner and hence cursed by God since he was blind, portrays the positive effects of experiencing God's unconditional love. Once cured of his blindness, he refuses to be intimidated as were his parents by the knowledgeable religious leaders who tried to limit God's all-embracing love.

The self-confidence he exhibits in face of their bullying makes it a fitting story with which to end this book.

Whether a person has discovered the faithfulness of God for the first time, or whether it be a rediscovery after a period of alienation, one is able to face life with a new vision that brings with it a kind of chain reaction. Like the blind man who was cured, trust that God accepts us and loves us just as we are generates growth in other areas of life also. Self-confidence is undergirded by trust in God's incontestable love which in turn enhances a person's ability to be oneself regardless of what others may think or say. The man who had his sight restored does not flinch at the queries about his being the one who used to sit and beg. He answers with an assurance that ridicule will not squelch: "I am the man" (Jn 9:8). When the religious leaders ask him a second time who it was that opened his eyes and how, he responds boldly and with self-confidence that he has already told them and they would not listen. "Why do you want to hear it again? Do you too want to become his disciples?" (Jn 9:27).

Experience of other people's love and acceptance generally builds self-esteem and consequently makes a person more lovable. Relationships with family, friends and acquaintances take on a newness that gives life to all involved. Sorrows, failures and disappointments can be shared with those we love just as freely as joys, successes and hopes. Life then becomes fully human and a silent invitation: "Come and see what God has done" (Ps 66:5).

Notes

❖   ❖   ❖

Chapter I: The Challenge

1. Robert L. Selman, *The Growth of Interpersonal Understanding* (New York: Academic Press, 1980) 79.

2. Alice Walker, *The Color Purple* (New York: Pocket Books, a division of Simon and Schuster, 1982).

3. Walker 199.

4. Albert Ellis and Robert Harper, *A New Guide to Rational Living* (Englewood Cliffs: Prentice-Hall, 1975) 88–195.

5. Ellis and Harper 168.

6. Walker 202.

7. Walker 203.

8. Walker 204.

9. Ibid.

10. F.W. Dillistone, *Christianity and Symbolism* (London: Collins Press, 1955) 291.

11. A.H. Maslow, *Motivation and Personality*, 2nd ed. (New York: Harper and Row, 1960).

12. George S. Spinks, *Psychology and Religion* (Boston: Beacon Press, 1963) 66.

13. Spinks 98.

14. Bonnidell Clouse, *Moral Development* (Grand Rapids: Baker Books, 1985) 31.

15. David Verner, *Household of God* (Atlanta: Scholar's Press, 1983) 45.

Chapter II: God Is Faithful in Loving Us

1. Joseph Fitzmyer, *The Gospel of Luke* (Anchor Bible 28 A; Garden City: Doubleday, 1985) 1221.
2. I.H. Marshall, *Commentary on Luke* (New Testament Greek Commentary; Grand Rapids: Eerdmans, 1978) 697.

Chapter III: God Is Faithful in Forgiving Us

1. Gerhard von Rad, *Genesis* (Louisville: Westminster Press, 1972) 134.
2. Bruce Vawter, *On Genesis* (New York: Doubleday, 1977) 120.
3. James A. Charlesworth, *The Old Testament Pseudepigrapha* (Garden City: Doubleday, 1983) 1:806: "Therefore the Lord made my catch to be an abundance of fish; for whoever shares with his neighbor receives a multitude from the Lord" (6:6).

Chapter IV: God Is Faithful in Caring for Us

1. Elisabeth Schüssler Fiorenza, *In Memory of Her* (New York: Crossroad, 1984) 126.
2. Walker 117.
3. G. Fohrer, "*soter*," *Theological Dictionary of the New Testament,* eds. G. Kittel and G. Friedrich, VII (Grand Rapids: Eerdmans, 1974) 970–980.
4. Raymond E. Brown, *The Gospel of John* (Anchor Bible 29; Garden City: Doubleday, 1966) 503.
5. Raymond E. Brown, *The Gospel and Epistles of John* (Collegeville: The Liturgical Press, 1988) 80.